THE SÁNDOR FERENCZI-

1921-1933

Edited and annotated by Christopher Fortune

Christopher Fortune holds a doctorate in the history of psycho-analysis from the University of Toronto. He has published and lectured internationally on Sándor Ferenczi and psychoanalysis. His articles, interviews and reviews on psychological and social issues have appeared in popular and scholarly journals, including *Psychology Today*, *The Village Voice* and *The British Journal of Psychotherapy*. He works as a child psychotherapist in Vancouver, Canada.

THE

SÁNDOR FERENCZI–GEORG GRODDECK

CORRESPONDENCE

1921-1933

Edited and annotated by Christopher Fortune

Translated by Jeannie Cohen, Elisabeth Petersdorff, Norbert Ruebsaat

OPEN GATE PRESS

incorporating Centaur Press (1954)

LONDON

First published in Great Britain in 2002 by Open Gate Press
51 Achilles Road, London NW6 1DZ

British Library Cataloguing-in-Publication Programme
A catalogue record for this book is available from the British Library.

ISBN 1 871871 44 1

Printed in Great Britain by
The Bath Press, Bath

CONTENTS

Preface

Of the early psychoanalysts, Sándor Ferenczi (1873-1933) was considered the most brilliant therapist – acknowledged by Freud to be a 'master of analysis'. Georg Groddeck (1866-1934), a German physician, was the source for Freud's concept of the 'Id' and has been referred to as the 'father of psychosomatic medicine'.

The correspondence, which consists primarily of Ferenczi's letters to Groddeck, provides important new insights into Ferenczi's professional and personal life. Different from his letters to Freud, whom he saw as a father-figure, Ferenczi pursued a more open friendship with Groddeck, as though he were a favourite older brother. They explored ideas, including self-analysis, mutual analysis, the body-mind relationship, and wrestled with the question of whether psychoanalysis could be a science. The letters resonate with critical theoretical and clinical issues today.

I have been researching and writing about Sándor Ferenczi for the past fifteen years, with a focus on his later work (1924-1933), which parallels the period of the Ferenczi-Groddeck correspondence. This research led to a number of publications, including reviews of Ferenczi's *Clinical Diary* (1932), and chapters on the clinical relationship with his important patient, Elizabeth Severn ('R.N.').[1] I have also presented papers on Ferenczi at international conferences in Budapest, Geneva, London, Paris and Versailles, and in Italy. In 1991, the psychoanalytic historian, Paul Roazen, approached me with the idea of editing an English edition of the correspondence; there already existed a French edition (1982), an Italian edition (1985), and a German edition (1986). In the spring of 1993, I was appointed by the Ferenczi estate as editor. Since that time, I have been searching for all existing letters, particularly for any of the missing Groddeck letters. My search for these letters has taken me to archives in Europe and North America, including Ferenczi archives in Paris and Budapest, Groddeck archives in Frankfurt (the Groddeck Society) and Freiburg, the Balint archives in Geneva, the British Psycho-Analytical Institute in London, and I communicated with the Fromm archive in Tübingen, the Fromm-Reichman group at Chestnut Lodge in Baltimore, the Library of Congress in Washington, and the Payne-Whitney Clinic in New York.

Assisted in my research by Ferenczi's executor, Paris psycho-analyst Dr Judith Dupont, and by the Georg Groddeck Society, four-teen of Ferenczi's unpublished letters and cards have come to light. Furthermore, three new letters and five unpublished postscripts by Ferenczi's wife, Gizella, have been located. However, sadly, up until now the search for Groddeck letters has uncovered only one new letter.

This new English edition supersedes the existing French, German and Italian editions,[2] which only had a typescript of the letters at their disposal. As a new work, this edition will be the most accurate and complete rendering of the Ferenczi-Groddeck letters in any language, not only due to the incorporation of the new letters, but also because facsimiles of the original handwritten letters were used in preparing this edition.

The publication of this correspondence in English is long overdue. Its proven importance to English-speaking scholars is confirmed by the fact that the French and German editions are regularly cited in English-language psychoanalytic literature. In addition, the French, German and Italian volumes were published with little detailed com-mentary or annotation. Sabourin (1985) noted this scholarly absence in his introduction to the earlier Ferenczi-Groddeck Correspondence editions. He writes: 'This exceptional document should have been accompanied by a detailed commentary of the context of the events.' This new English edition, for the first time in any language, provides comprehensive editorial annotations, many based on new research, which give the necessary background and context to the corre-spondence. In editing this new volume the annotations of the earlier editions were used as resource material and, where appropriate, incorporated into the new notes. This volume also corrects mistakes and omissions found in the earlier French, German and Italian edi-tions.[3]

The literature on Sándor Ferenczi's work and life is rapidly grow-ing, as many of his controversial ideas on the analytic relationship, early trauma, and countertransference, are enthusiastically redis-covered and debated after being suspended – and in some cases repressed by the psychoanalytic establishment – for more than seventy years.

The recent publication of his 1932 *Clinical Diary*, and the long-awaited three-volume Freud-Ferenczi correspondence, confirms Ferenczi's significance to Freud, and reveals his innovative contributions central to present-day psychoanalysis and psychotherapy. Ferenczi's 1933 paper, 'Confusion of tongues', which has long been recognized as an underground classic on child sexual abuse, is finally being accorded the historical recognition it deserves, both within and beyond psychoanalysis.

This volume not only provides an important and missing piece of Sándor Ferenczi scholarship, but re-introduces Georg Groddeck, a fascinating and timely psycho-medical figure, to an English-speaking audience. Widely published in German and French, Georg Groddeck's work is attracting increasing interest. Negotiations are presently under way for a number of his works to be published in English, including the republication of his classic, *The Book of the It* (1923).

These letters offer a unique historical perspective on psychoanalysis beyond Ernest Jones's orthodox views of Ferenczi, Groddeck, and even Freud. As a record of an intimate friendship between two passionate and original thinkers – at times Freud's followers, at other times, analytic dissidents – these letters capture the adventurous spirit of the early years of the psychoanalytic movement and will resonate with readers, both inside and outside psychoanalysis.

Christopher Fortune

---

[1] See Fortune (1993, 1994, 1996).

[2] These editions are different only in the translation; the editing and annotations are the same.

[3] The original facsimiles allowed for the correction of misdated letters, mistranscriptions, missing words and passages, and frequent underlining of words by Ferenczi.

Acknowledgements

From its inception, this book has taken ten years to appear in print. For different stages in its development, I would like to acknowledge the following:

I am grateful for the assistance of a grant-in-aid from the *Hannah Institute for the History of Medicine*, Toronto, and a Doctoral Fellowship of the *Social Sciences and Research Council of Canada*.

Norbert Ruebsaat for his most helpful work on a first draft translation.

The Department of Applied Psychology – University of Toronto (O.I.S.E./UT). My doctoral committee: Professor Morris Eagle, Prof. Andrew Brink, Prof. Otto Weininger and Prof. Donald Carveth; Prof. Edward Shorter and Vivienne Pasika and family.

Prof. Paul Roazen, who suggested this project to me.

Mark Paterson and Associates for their patient and persistent work as literary agents.

In Paris, Judith Dupont, Ferenczi's literary executor, for her support over many years, her availability and insights as a consultant, her hospitality and her generous access to Ferenczi's archives.

Le Coq-Heron Translation Group, Paris, for their original translation and editorial work on the first volumes of the correspondence in French, German and Italian.

Sándor Ferenczi scholars for their interest, support and at times editorial help: André Haynal; Ernst Falzeder – for specific help on some historical details; Eva Brabant – for specific ideas on Ferenczi and Groddeck; Franco Borgogno, Carlo Bonomi, Axel and Peter Hoffer, and Judy Vida.

The *Georg Groddeck-Gesellschaft*, Frankfurt, especially Beate Schuh for her kind and unfailing support and for providing access to invaluable materials of the Groddeck archive; Herbert Will for generously offering copies of the original Ferenczi letters; Otto Jägersberg for his passionate archival work on Groddeck; Groddeck's committed publisher K. D. Wolff of *Stroemfeld Verlag*, and the late Margaretha Honegger, Groddeck's former secretary and literary executor for over fifty years.

In Vancouver: for their loyal support, my mother Ruth Fortune, my father, John C. Fortune, Prof. John Allan, Julia Day-Lavelle, Margaret Severn, Peter Lipskis, Bonnie Fordyce, Christine Cohen Park, Anna St. Keverne, Cortez Island.

Independent scholars: Peter Swales, Russell Jacoby, and Jery Zaslove.

Papers based on this correspondence were presented at Congresses of the International Association for the History of Psychoanalysis in Paris (1996), and Versailles (2000) – (President: Alain de Mijolla); and through the auspices of Peter Rudnytsky at the Group for the Application of Psychology, University of Florida (1997), and an International Colloquy sponsored by Assistencia y Estudios Psicologicos Argentinos (Buenos Aires) in Collalbo (Bolzano), Italy, 1995, (Fabiana Musri, translator).

Mike Moskowitz, publisher, of *The Other Press*, New York.

Finally, I would like to acknowledge the careful, expert and painstaking editorial work of Elisabeth Petersdorff, and the fine, supportive and friendly ongoing editorial guidance of the project by Jeannie Cohen – both of *Open Gate Press*.

And, in the end, my son Hugh Fordyce-Fortune, a wise child, for perspective, delight and inspiration.

Christopher Fortune

Introduction

THE SOURCES OF CREATIVITY

> *However, it is good to study other people's*
> *inventions in a way which reveals to us the*
> *sources of creativity, and which makes them*
> *somehow our own.*
>
> G. W. Leibniz to L. Bourguet
>
> (Leibniz: *Die Philosophischen Schriften*, ed. C. Gerhardt,
> Vol. 3, Correspondence 1709–1716, p.568)

When publishing the private correspondence of an important person in history, philosophy, arts and letters or science – unless it concerns people who lived in centuries past – one always encounters many difficulties, some of them anticipated, others unpredictable.

However, it seems that time does not remove all problems, since the thousands of letters written by Louis XI, and preserved, had never been worked on, or even read, before the contemporary historian Paul Murray Kendall did so, and as far as I know, they have not been published even now. It seems that reading someone's private correspondence demands a serious effort on the part of the reader, an inner movement towards the author, one made from interest and sympathy, or rather from empathy and identification, as well as from human respect, rather than that respect which we feel before greatness and qualities of character. It is not always easy to mobilise such sentiments in oneself; it is easier to pass judgements. The fact is that the publication of any private correspondence is always preceded by long and laborious negotiation with the families of the author and the recipient – negotiations which often end with an incomplete publication of the letters, and even with incomplete letters – sometimes without the omissions even being pointed out. However, as we regularly meet reservations of this sort, we must acknowledge that there are numerous and powerful reasons for them.

The immediate argument is one of discretion: we do not have the right to divulge information which was communicated in confidence to a particular person at a particular moment, and which might embarrass, upset or disturb someone else, unless given express authorisation by the people concerned or by their descendants. This seems convincing and reasonable. However, the question then arises: should we therefore refrain from making any revelation which might call into question the image which the family or friends might want to present of their great man, even if it means deceiving and misleading those who are doing their best to understand him and to work with his discoveries? By blurring the trail leading towards 'the sources of creativity', do we not become guilty of a sort of falsification of the vital work of the very person whose memory we want to protect? In the first of his *Psychoanalytic Notebooks*, Charles Baudouin quotes these words of Freud: '... A work's fate does not rest entirely on itself, but is also in the hands of those who want to represent it and promote it. Where will they take it?' By changing the picture of the relationship which exists between a man and his work – even for the best reasons in the world – do we not commit a sort of abuse against a legacy which is due to humanity? So even this apparently simple and obvious argument about discretion raises many problems; it was often invoked in relation to the correspondence between Freud and Ferenczi, many passages of which correspond to a real analytic session. Here is what Marthe Robert has to say on the subject in her preface to the volume of correspondence between Freud and Arnold Zweig, which was severely expurgated by their two sons, Ernest Freud and Adam Zweig: 'Here, as always, the subject of the scandal is, it seems, the analysis – not the analysis which has long since become an accepted part of culture, but analysis as personal encounter and experience of the dangers inherent in it with regard to conventional prejudice and to what is permissible.'

A correspondence does not only bring revelations and clarifications. It also brings new problems, new sources of error. A letter implies a relationship between two people at a given moment and in a precise context. It only takes on its whole meaning in that context. Part of its meaning will, therefore, elude every reader except the one to whom it was sent, and it follows inevitably that there will be some errors of interpretation, or even misrepresentations, on the part of the reader or commentator.

As well as this, any selection which is made from letters, or passages for publication, introduces a note of falsehood: for it will necessarily be made according to the desires, reservations, inhibitions or personal ethics of the selector. He may even act with the sincere conviction that by his selection he is serving the author's work, reputation or message, by avoiding the possibility that hasty, superficial or malicious commentators might seize upon this or that phrase or passage and use it to cast suspicion on the author or on his entire work.

Naturally, the closer the correspondents are to us, the more topical, lively and influential their work will be and the more understandable the reservations will be. But here again, things are less straight-forward than they appear: we could take the view that giving back a voice to deceased people whose work still has all its inspirational strength, and not leaving them entirely to the mercy of their heirs, disciples, successors, commentators and users, might actually be of benefit to their work, even on the occasions when it might harm their established reputation. This line of argument is brought to bear against those who think that it is enough to wait for passions to quieten down, and for historical perspective to set in: but is this not the same thing as waiting for the whole inspirational charge of the work to fade away? It reminds us of Daumier's painting in which the prosecutor stands in front of a dying man stretched out on a prison pallet, and says to the gaoler: 'We can free that man, he's no longer dangerous.'

There seems always to be a moment of uneasiness during the 'passage to posterity' in the course of which a human being is trans-formed into an historical figure. This is what is known in literature as 'purgatory'. In the course of this transmutation, the author, as human being, is expected to keep quiet and be discreet, so as not to embarrass the work of development being wrought by the new gen-eration, which needs sages and heroes rather than crotchety grand-fathers complaining of their pains and their moods. It is far from unusual for people to experience a sort of liberation at the death of one of these loved and revered beings, for whom they have reserved a place in their personal pantheon: once the conflicts and problems they had with them have been extinguished, they can finally love them in peace, without their irritating traits constantly intruding on that love.

Once centuries have passed, things are quite different. Of course the works of great men of the past – of philosophers, poets, scholars, etc. – can move us and leave their mark on us as individuals, but they do not have an active hold over our times. They have given what they could, they have perhaps even left their imprint on a culture, but they are no longer bubbling in ferment. Of course, there are some exceptions: let's imagine that we find the private diaries of Jesus and want to publish them, the likelihood is that this would pose enormous problems for a good number of individuals and organisations. Jesus has become a public good, a protected monument, common property, and if he came and imposed himself now, with his real personality, and challenged the tranquil enjoyment of that public property which he has become, it would not be easily accepted. We may remember the epilogue of Bernard Shaw's *St. Joan*: when Joan has been rehabilitated, canonised and worshipped, and proposes to come back, everyone – both friends and enemies, her contemporaries and ours – cries out and begs her not to come and complicate their lives.

Other, more profound, sentiments can also play a part in determining people's attitudes towards highly personal revelations about the dead. The feelings we experience towards the dead are rather ambivalent. On the one hand, we treat them with great respect and consideration. Their body is the object of rites and ceremonies, we make a funeral oration over them, and – at least for a certain time – we respect their last wishes. Let them rest in peace, we say ... and let them leave us in peace. All the same, once they are freed from the everyday events and passions of life, we think of them as having acquired wisdom and power. So we are keen to invoke them and try to make them speak. But what we do not want is for them to show themselves on their own initiative: that causes panic, and we have to banish, exorcise and send back the recalcitrant soul quickly to a more discreet and more definitive death. We should not forget that death is a contagious disease. A too-human outburst over a very recent death evokes in us a host of insufficiently mastered fears.

Naturally, we find all this going on in the attitudes of groups – and particularly scientific ones – towards their founders. The psychoanalytic group is no exception in this respect. And the fact that psychoanalysis works on, and with, the passions, does not weaken this process.

In addition, in the case of psychoanalysis, there is yet another element that comes into play which gives today's analytic groups the incentive to exert as much control as they can over the fermentations which their ancestors might yet spark off *a posteriori*. After all, psychoanalysis was a genuine revolution; it turned almost every area of science, arts, education, etc., upside down, and left a significant mark on its – that is, our – age. The founders of psychoanalysis were aware of this. They often spoke of the 'psychoanalytic movement'. To maintain and defend this movement, one of them, Sándor Ferenczi, recommended that an organisation should be created: the International Association of Psychoanalysis. This was no anodyne proposal; it carried risks. An organisation is a valuable tool in the struggle, but it never furthers progress, even though it does not always impede it.

No revolution escapes from the temptation – or perhaps the necessity – to organise and institutionalise its conquests, to make them secure and to prevent any backsliding. But thus every sort of mobility – whether forwards or backwards – often finds itself compromised. Another consequence of the process of organisation is that gradually, yet inevitably, revolutionary temperaments are replaced by organisational temperaments.

There is no doubt that Ferenczi had a revolutionary temperament. He was ideally suited to the combative and conquering attitude of the first psychoanalysts, whose vocabulary is most revealing. All their talk is of 'struggling' for the 'cause' by equipping themselves with an 'arsenal' of effective 'weapons' to confound the adversary.

And it was Ferenczi, one of the most revolutionary and one of the least organisational of the members of the analytic community, who none the less proposed the foundation of an international psychoanalytic association, in which he saw a logistical basis for the psychoanalytic 'movement'.

However, when we re-read the article he wrote in 1911,[1] where he sets out his proposal, we realise that he did not make it naively. He starts by giving his reasons for making this proposal, and we may notice several which have a rather ambivalent ring. Then he examines the potential consequences, both those which he hopes for, and those which he would prefer to avoid.

He writes the following about psychoanalysts:

'... they too had to, and still have to, conduct guerilla warfare, just as the pioneers in the New World did ... lacking authority, discipline and leading strings ...'

He is fully aware that:

'There was actually one type of human being who was won over by this 'irregular' type of work; I refer to people of artistic gifts, who were led into our camp partly because of their intuitive understanding of the problems with which we were concerned, but were also attracted by our rebellion against scientific scholasticism ...'

But:

'Disadvantages as well as advantages, however, gradually emerged

THE SOURCES OF CREATIVITY

from this guerrilla warfare. The complete lack of any central direction meant that in some cases particular scientific and personal interests got the better of and acted detrimentally to the common interest, what I should like to call the "central idea" ...'

Elsewhere he observes that:

'... while a very valuable and talented section of society is attracted to us precisely because of our lack of organisation, the majority, who are accustomed to order and discipline, draw from our irregularity only new material for resistance. Finally, we should not forget those timid people who approve of us while yet being hesitant about joining us as an individual among individuals, but who would be entirely well-disposed to joining an organisation.'

Ferenczi appears to have been under no illusion about the sort of disciples psychoanalysis could attract if it presented an image of order and discipline. In this article he gives the impression of pleading against one part of himself. He tries to curb his own revolutionary impulses for the 'good of the cause' by proposing to the analysts that they should give themselves structures of respectability.

Then he continues:

'I know the excrescences that grow from organized groups, and I am aware that in most political, social and scientific organizations childish megalomania, vanity, admiration of empty formalities, blind obedience, or personal egoism prevail instead of quiet, honest work in the general interest.'

Comparing the structure of associations to that of the family, he expresses a wish:

'[This association] ... would be a family in which the father enjoyed no dogmatic authority, but only that to which he was entitled by reason of his abilities and labours. His pronouncements would not be followed blindly, as if they were divine revelations, but, like every-thing else, would be subject to thoroughgoing criticism, which he would accept, not with the absurd superiority of the paterfamilias, but with the attention that it deserved.

   Moreover, the older and younger children united in this association would accept being told the truth to their face, however bitter and sobering it might be, without childish sensitivity and vindictiveness.'

Apparently, Ferenczi was well aware of the enormity of these demands, because he prudently adds:

'In the present state of civilization, i.e. in the second century of surgical anaesthesia, it can be taken for granted that we should endeavour to tell the truth without causing unnecessary pain ...'

However, he thinks that he can hope for the establishment of

'... an association in which people can tell each other the truth, in which people's real capacities can be recognized without envy ...'

Towards the end of the article, he again specifies in a few phrases what he hopes for from an organisation, despite the risks which he has just enumerated:

'... an association, membership of which would offer some guarantee that Freud's own psycho-analytic methods were being used ... One of the special tasks of the association would be to unmask the scientific looting to which psycho-analysis is subject to-day. Careful sifting of new members would make it possible to separate the wheat from the chaff. The association should be content with a small membership rather than accept or retain people who are not firmly convinced on matters of principle.'

All of us will have our own views on how far the formation of the association has fulfilled the tasks which Ferenczi assigned to it, and avoided the pitfalls he mentioned – and at what price. Certainly, psychoanalysis has won the battle for respectability. But every benefit comes with a price tag; and what was the price of respectability? In trying to evaluate this, more than one reader of Ferenczi's work has asked himself whether or not Ferenczi would succeed in getting himself admitted into a psychoanalytic association today, and whether his training analysis would be acceptable ...

The fact is that Ferenczi – who, we should remember, was never President of the International Psychoanalytic Association whose creation he recommended – was excluded for a long time from the training programmes of most of the psychoanalytic schools. In France, his work was little read, and rarely studied. It was not until 35 years after his death that the first volume of his complete works appeared in French, and nearly half a century passed before the fourth and final volume was published. As far as his personal writings are concerned, there are still many problems to resolve.

Several decades of hesitation and discussion preceded the decision to publish his clinical diary of the year 1932, and his correspondence with Groddeck, published here, spent a long time in a drawer. As to the copious correspondence between Freud and Ferenczi, which they carried on without a break from 1908 to 1933 despite all the differences which must have occurred between them, the various obstacles to its publication took a long time to be resolved, and perhaps cannot even now be entirely clearly formulated. For a start, there is a legal period of fifty years [now 70], increased by the years of war, which protects writings from any untimely publication, unless the author's heirs give permission. Freud's heirs seem to have been hesitant about the publication of the letters between him and Ferenczi, and had even more reservations about an unabridged edition of these letters. To date, it has not been possible to publish any of the exchanges of letters between Freud and his correspondents in its entirety; as to the letters written to Ferenczi, only some have been published, in Jones's biography of Freud, or at random in articles.[2] Interestingly, we do not find the same reticence among Ferenczi's heirs. His personality must have something to do with it: he was open throughout his life: in his articles, lectures and personal contacts; and he rejected any idea of building himself a façade. This is perhaps the very reason why he is less vulnerable after his death. He gives the impression of being a man who above all wanted to be loved and of thinking that the best way to achieve this was to reveal himself. Ferenczi's heirs have adopted the same attitude. From as early as 1946, Gizella Ferenczi, Sándor's widow, asked her husband's literary executor, Michael Bálint, to negotiate the publication of his correspondence with the Freud family. He devoted himself to this – without success – until his death in 1970. The attitudes of the various people responsible allow us to guess at a number of secret, painful and anxiety-ridden motives, which are no doubt largely unconscious and the more powerful for that. The fear of leaving the floor to great people whose every phrase still arouses resonances which are new and unexpected – and for that reason completely uncontrollable – certainly plays a part in this.

Institutions defend themselves against those who might disturb them. And Ferenczi is one of those: he creates disturbance by his theories, his researches and his experiments, by the liberties which he allows himself in his thoughts as well as in his practice, by his whole being. The profound impact which he had on psychoanalysis is conveyed by the scale of the methods – neglect, devaluation, disregard, inappropriate over-simplification – employed by the psychoanalytic community to protect themselves from it, until they are ready to maybe receive it. They even had recourse to a means which it is surprising to encounter among professional explorers of the human psyche: in the third volume of his monumental biography of Freud, Ernest Jones dismisses the entire work of Ferenczi's last years as being the work of a sick mind and thus being of no interest. This judgement, which was refuted over and over again by those who knew Ferenczi (Bálint, Hermann, Dr Levy, who was his family doctor, etc.) and which was never corroborated by any witness, was nevertheless given remarkable credence in the psychoanalytic community, and even today analysts can be found who hold this view.[3]

The correspondence published here raises the same problems as all the others: the correspondents deal with the most personal matters, mention aspects of their past which have never been mentioned, and betray their weaknesses and their faults. Nevertheless, as we indicated above, it is perhaps because of the personalities of the two men in question that this correspondence is able to be published in its entirety: we essentially have here the letters of the 'enfant terrible of psychoanalysis' to the 'wild analyst'. For their part, everybody knows what to expect. Only three letters of Groddeck have been preserved, two addressed to Sándor, and one to Gizella Ferenczi after the death of her husband.[4]

Mrs Margaretha Honegger, the executor of Georg Groddeck's will, was willing to put copies of this correspondence, of which she retains the originals, at our disposal. We owe to her good offices the authorisation to publish the letters of Groddeck, and thank her for this.[5] We should also like to express our gratitude to Maria Torok who helped us with her knowledge throughout our work, and also to Alice Székely-Kovács who sent us the letters of Frédéric Kovács published in the appendix.

The correspondence between Ferenczi and Groddeck covers a period of 12 years, from April 1921 to March 1933. The reader is immediately struck by the speed with which Ferenczi passes from 'Most honoured colleague' (Sehr geehrter Herr Kollege) on 17th August 1921 to 'Dear Friend' (Lieber Freund) at Christmas the same year, then to 'Dear Groddeck' on 27th February 1922. Groddeck starts his letter of 12th November 1922 with 'Dear Sándor', to which Ferenczi replies with a 'Dear Georg' on 11th December. These two men, who were of such different origins and who had developed intellectually in such different ways, seem genuinely to have been made to understand one another.

Both of them, each in his own way, were out-of-the-ordinary personalities. Groddeck openly proclaimed his marginal position in relation to the psychoanalytic movement by proclaiming proudly at the Berlin meeting: 'I am a wild psychonalyst.' Ferenczi, on the other hand, suffered from feeling marginalised because of the originality of his thought and technique. He was hurt by the nickname he had been given of '*enfant terrible* of psychoanalysis', and was always repeating, with the greatest insistence, that both his theoretical ideas and his technical ways were entirely consonant with the most classical psychoanalysis. In his desire to be accepted, particularly by Freud, he never missed an opportunity to emphasise the scientific contributions of his colleagues. This is how he found the seeds of his active technique in certain passages of Freud, and gave him the credit for it. We know how rare such an attitude is among scientists, including psychoanalysts.

In addition to the marginality which both experienced in their own ways, other circumstances might also have brought the two men together: both considered themselves basically to be doctors, and wanted to care for people and cure them. Groddeck did not think it absolutely essential to understand what he was doing once his patient was feeling better.[6] Ferenczi constantly sought to gain a greater and better understanding: he always insisted that it was not sick people who ought to be selected according to their analyzability with the existing analytic technique, but the technique itself that should be modified, adapted and developed according to the needs of sick people.

What is more, both of them were perfectly aware that through the analyses an analyst conducts, he continues to analyse himself, and not just with the aim of achieving professional conscientiousness, but to cure himself. In the letter which Ferenczi writes to Groddeck on 11th October 1922, he alludes for the first time to the idea of mutual analysis – originally an idea of Groddeck's – which he was to develop in his clinical diary of 1932. Groddeck had for some time been pursuing a similar enterprise in his 'lectures to the sick' which were an integral part of the treatment he gave them, and in the course of which he spoke abundantly about himself.

At this time, when psychoanalysis was young, many analysts practised some kind of mutual analysis, which took the place of a training analysis. Intimate and analytic conversations alternated with exchanges of correspondence, as for example the letter from Ferenczi to Groddeck of 25th December 1921, or that of Groddeck to Ferenczi of 12th November 1922. But apart, of course, from

Ferenczi, no one had tried to systematise and define the process. As a rule, the practice was rigorously rejected when it concerned the analysis of a patient, and it is even more firmly rejected today. But if we cast a critical eye over certain attitudes or interventions which we may see in the course of many analyses, certain indiscretions, explanations or awkwardnesses which occasionally occur, or even the deliberate interpretations of counter-transference – not to speak of institutional psychotherapy – we wonder whether mutual analysis might not deserve to be studied in more depth, rather than being rejected out of hand as a heresy. As for Ferenczi, he had the habit of calling things by their name once he had discovered them.

Although there were many things which might have brought Ferenczi and Groddeck together – for example, both men had felt themselves to be unloved during their childhood – there were also important differences between them, and divergences which sometimes made themselves very painfully felt. They came from totally opposite backgrounds: the Groddeck family, conventional, traditionalist, Christian, was in full decline; Georg, the youngest, was practically its only survivor. The Ferenczis, Jewish intellectuals, liberals, who had started from nothing, were socially well on the upward path.

From documents and personal statements gathered by Michael Bálint for a biography of Ferenczi which he did not have time to write, we know that Bernát Ferenczi and Rosa Eibenschütz had 12 children, all born in Miskolcz in Hungary, where Bernát was a bookseller and printer. According to the birth certificates provided by the civil state registry of the Israelite Consistory of Miskolcz, these children were:

1. Henrik, born on 27th March 1860.
   Bernát Ferenczi started his family rather late. Born in 1830, he was thirty when his first child was born. At this time, the young Sigmund Freud was nearly four years old.
2. Max (Miksa), born on 19th March 1861.
3. Zsigmond (Sigmund!), born on 17th March 1862.
   He was Sándor's favourite brother.
4. Ilona (Helen), born on 30th September 1865.
5. Rebus (perhaps a diminutive of Rebecca), born 24th April, 1868.
   Her name was later changed to 'Maria'. This was not the only name-change in the Ferenczi family, as we shall see.

The young Groddeck, born between Ilona and Rebus, was by this time one and a half.

6. Jakab (Jack), known as Joseph, born on 14th July 1869.
7. Gizella, born on 8th June 1872.
   Sándor's future wife, also older than him, but by eight years, was also called Gizella.
8. Sándor (Alexander), born on 7th July 1873.
   By this time, the young Sigmund Freud was 17, and Georg Groddeck was 7.
9. Moritz Károly, born on 17th February 1877.
10. Vilma, born on 3rd June 1878.
    She died very young, before her first birthday, of diphtheria, according to some accounts, but there is no confirmation of this. It has been said that Sándor, who was 4 years old by this time, would have forgotten that this sister had ever existed, but this seems rather unlikely.
11. Lajos (Louis), born on 6th September 1879.
12. Zsófia (Sophie), born on 18th July 1883.

The birth certificates of the 12 Ferenczi children tell the tale of a whole succession of name changes, sometimes as a result of official decrees, sometimes from usage, sometimes from civil servants' slips of the pen. When Henrik, the oldest, was born, the father is called Baruch Fränkel, and the mother Rosi Eibensatz. A year later, when Max was born, the father appears under the name Bernát (Bernard) Frenkel, and the mother under that of Rosa Eibenschütz (her real name, mangled in the first version by the civil servant). So the father had changed his Jewish first name for a contemporary Hungarian one. The fifth child, a daughter, received the first name Rebus, a strange first name which may have been a Hungarian diminutive for Rebecca, and which was changed later, at an unknown date, to 'Maria' by official decree. In 1879, the father's name, which had passed from Fränkel to Frenkel or Fraenkel, becomes Ferenci, also by official decree, and the names of all the children were modified as a consequence, with the exception of Vilma's, as she had died before that date. Only Zsófia, born in 1883, has her name from the beginning. Gradually, usage would add a 'z', and the name would become definitively 'Ferenczi'.

Mrs Magda Ferenczi (the younger daughter of Gizella – Sándor's wife – but also the wife of Lajos Ferenczi, Sándor's younger brother), has brought the following point to our attention: Baruch-Bernát Fränkel-Frenkel-Fraenkel, a volunteer fighter in the insurrection of 1848, was offered the name 'Ferenczy', written with a 'y', a sign of nobility in Hungary. A staunch democrat, he refused, and became Ferenci, then Ferenczi, a commoner's name.

Perhaps a minute study of Ferenczi's articles and letters would allow us to discover the effect which all these changes of name – all contributing to a break with his origins – had on his sense of identity.

What do we know about Sándor's parents? According to Zsófia, the younger sister of Sándor, Bernát Ferenczi (at that time, Baruch Fränkel) was born in Poland, at Cracow, in 1830. He emigrated to Hungary at a time and for reasons which we do not know (but which, given the conditions in Poland at that time, might well have been racial), and in 1848, at the age of 18, he took part in the Hungarian insurrection against Austrian domination, in which insurrection the poet Sándor Petöfi was hero and martyr, killed in combat at the age of 25. This insurrection, which at first looked certain to triumph, was finally defeated and harshly suppressed. Some twenty years later, in 1868, it would lead to the constitution of an independent kingdom of Hungary, within Austro-Hungary.

After the failure of the insurrection, Bernát first went to live at Eger, then at Miskolcz, where he became manager of the bookshop of Michael Heilprin, an American citizen; the bookshop was situated at Széchényi utca 13. This same Heilprin was – according to Ferenczi family legend – the secretary of Lajos Kossuth, one of the principal leaders of the insurrection of 1848-9. In 1856, when Michael Heilprin decided to return to America, Bernát Fränkel bought the bookshop from him. In order to be able to make this purchase, he had to present certificates of his moral standards (perhaps because of his foreign origins, or maybe because of his participation in the insurrection, which at that time was not yet an officially recognised claim to fame). One of the certificates, dated 5th March 1856, was signed by Chérubin Chavola, the director of the town's Catholic College; the other was signed by Gustav Heckenast, bookshop owner and publisher, who was famous for having printed on his presses on 15th March 1848 (which has since become the Hungarian national festival) the celebrated poem of Sándor Petöfi: 'Stand up, Magyar!' By a curious coincidence, the certificate is dated 6th May 1856, the very day on which Sigmund Freud was born. The bookshop remained in the ownership of the Ferenczi family for about a hundred years, until the nationalisation of businesses after the 1939-45 War.

Rosa Eibenschütz, Sándor's mother, was born on 11th December 1840. According to her grandson Ladislas Vajda, the son of Rebus-Maria, she was born at Cracow or at Tarnov, but the family soon moved to Vienna. The Eibenschütz house in Vienna still belonged to that family in 1969, when Mr Vajda gave his account to Michael Bálint.

Bernát and Rosa married in 1858, probably in Vienna. Their first child, Henrik, was born in 1860, that is, when Rosa was not quite twenty years old. By 22, she would be the mother of three children – and there would still be nine to come – but it seems that Rosa was a strong woman and perfectly capable of dealing with such a situation.

As the family bookshop had prospered, Bernát soon added a printing works, and then a concert agency. He then went on to organise concerts himself. His house became a meeting-place for artists and intellectuals from Hungary and from abroad. Animated discussions took place there, and the family played chamber music together. Bernát was a respected person in the town. On 24th September 1876, he became vice-president of the 1848 Veterans' Association. In 1880, he was unanimously elected President of the Chamber of Commerce at Miskolcz.

Magda Ferenczi gives an idyllic description of the family life led by the Ferenczis in their first-floor flat over the bookshop: it was an hospitable open house with an intellectually stimulating atmosphere, where gaiety and the greatest freedom held sway. The children could invite their friends and go out as they wished. It seems, however, that Sándor did not enjoy this family atmosphere, as his letter of 25th December 1921 shows, when he complains to Groddeck about the coldness and the lack of tenderness which prevailed there, as well as the excess of modesty and self-control which was demanded from the children.

According to Zsófia, his younger sister, Sándor was the favourite of his father, who gladly took him with him on the daily visits which he made to the vineyard which he owned in the neighbourhood.

Bernát Ferenczi died in 1888, when Sándor was 15 years old. Rosa, decidedly a wife in control, took over the running of the bookshop and printing press, and managed them successfully. She even opened a branch in Nyíregyháza. She also had a certain status in the town: she was President of the Union of Jewish Women. Mrs Ferenczi managed the family business until her son Károly had reached an age at which he could take it over. He continued this work until 1944, when he was deported.

Most of the children of Bernát and Rosa who reached adulthood married and had children; however, very few of them survived the deportations of the Second World War. Curiously, the only family which kept the name of Ferenczi is that of the adopted daughter of Zsiga (Sigmund, Sándor's favourite brother), who had married a German officer by the name of Richter. One of their sons, a doctor, went on to take legal steps to acquire the name Ferenczi.

The young Sándor was a brilliant student at the Protestant College in his town, like all his brothers. Then he went to Vienna to study medicine. All the details of his university degree course are fully known, thanks to the researches which Mrs Elfriede Pillinger made for Michael Bálint.

During his studies in Vienna, Sándor lived with one of his father's older brothers, his uncle Sigmund Fränkel (a highly significant first name in Sándor's life). His mother's family also lived in this city. During the same time, his favourite brother, Sigmund, worked as a chemical engineer in a paper-mill at Bruck-an-der-Mur, a little town north of Graz.[7] The two brothers adored mountaineering and frequently went climbing together.

Sándor obtained his medical diploma in 1894. Then he left to do his military service in the Austro-Hungarian army. After his service, he went to settle in Budapest. In 1897-98, he worked at the Rókus Hospital. On 24th July 1898 he became assistant doctor at the hospice for the poor and for prostitutes. Finally, in 1900, he set himself up as a neurologist. After a first reading of *The Interpretation of Dreams*, which did not immediately engage his support, he eventually made contact with Freud in 1908, and their relationship very rapidly developed into an enduring and lasting friendship, grievously troubled towards the end by divergences arising from Ferenczi's technical experiments, although the roots of this discontent went no doubt much further back in time and were much more deeply embedded. Their correspondence will allow us to understand what really passed between them. Nevertheless, however painful their divergence, it never resulted in a rupture, as the last letter from Ferenczi to Groddeck shows.[8]

Ferenczi, then, started practising psychoanalysis in 1908. He was

35 years old. In 1910, he became an expert advisor in court cases. He resigned from this post after the First World War.

He had known the family of the woman who would become his wife for a long time, because Gizella Altschul came to live in Miskolcz after her marriage to Géza Pálos. The relationship between Sándor and Gizella started in 1900. Gizella Pálos had two daughters: Elma and Magda. It appears (from the later account given by Elma) that Gizella's husband Géza Pálos, tolerated the relationship between Sándor and his wife, but did not want a divorce. However, he finally agreed to a divorce, and Sándor married Gizella on 1st March 1919. Pálos died of a heart attack on the very day of their wedding. They learned the news when they arrived at the town hall.

Sándor was 46 years old, Gizella 54. Before their marriage there was a painful episode which is mentioned in this correspondence: in 1911, Sándor fell desperately in love with Elma, Gizella's older daughter, then aged 24, and wanted to marry her.[9] Gizella was prepared to step aside and Sándor became engaged to Elma. After many ups and downs in which love, psychoanalysis, friendship and affection all played their part in turn, the engagement was broken off and the marriage to Gizella took place, under the sombre auspices which have just been described. However, the three participants would remain deeply affected by this episode.

During the First World War, Sándor was mobilised as a military doctor at Pápa, in Hungary. We know that while he was there he was visited by Freud. One day, he coughed up blood and was immediately sent to a sanatorium on the Semmering. The incident proved not to be serious, but it was at the root of one of those great hypochondriacal crises which Ferenczi would suffer from throughout his life. In the account she gave to Michael Bálint, Zsófia Ferenczi explains the incident as a simple wound which Sándor inflicted on his throat while he was swallowing something. Whatever it was, there is no doubt that it was the origin of the erroneous information according to which Ferenczi had a tubercular episode.

After the abdication of Charles I, Emperor of Austria and King of Hungary (as Charles IV) in November 1918, Hungary experienced several months of a liberal republican regime under the presidency of Count Michel Károlyi. During this time the writer and journalist Hugo Ignotus, himself a liberal, and a long-standing friend of Ferenczi, managed to have a Chair of Psychoanalysis, the first of its kind, created for Ferenczi at the university. Some time was needed to organise things, and in the meantime, in March 1919, the liberal republic gave way to the Soviet republic under the presidency of Béla Kun. The Chair of Psychoanalysis which he held during the brief Hungarian Commune, and also his Jewish origins, were to bring Ferenczi innumerable troubles in their wake under the reactionary regime of Horthy. In the end, he was even excluded from the Hungarian Medical Association.

Rosa, Sándor's mother, died in 1921, the very year in which he and Groddeck became friends and in which he spoke so bitterly of his family in the long Christmas day letter.

When the correspondence between Ferenczi and Groddeck began, Ferenczi was 48 years old and had been married for two years. He started to experiment with his active technique. He would criticise it himself from 1926 onwards, and would abandon it, to the benefit of the technique referred to as indulgence and relaxation.[10]

Ferenczi took a number of cures at Baden-Baden, at Groddeck's 'satanarium', as his patients liked to call it; he stayed there practically every year, accompanied by his wife, and he sent all his friends and relatives there, particularly Elma, the woman to whom he had briefly been engaged.

However, his health was in continual decline, until pernicious anaemia was finally diagnosed. Ferenczi died on 22th May 1933; he was, however, still able to congratulate Freud on his 77th birthday, on May 6th – the last letter he sent to Freud.

Judith Dupont

[1] 'On the organization of the psychoanalytic movement', *Final Contributions to the Problems and Methods of Psychoanalysis*, Brunner/Mazel, New York 1980, pp.299-307.

[2] Since the publication of this introduction in 1982, the whole Freud-Fliess correspondence, the Freud-Jung letters, and the Freud-Ferenczi letters have been published.

[3] See the important paper of Carlo Bonomi in the *International Journal of Psychoanalysis* (1999) 80, pp.507-542, 'Jones's Allegation of Ferenczi's Mental Deterioration Reconsidered'.

[4] A further letter from Groddeck to Ferenczi has been found since the publication of this introduction and is included in this edition.

[5] The new letters and cards, and copies of all the original cards and letters, which augment this present volume, were generously put at our disposal by the Groddeck Gesellschaft of Frankfurt (Beate Schuh, Herbert Will, Otto Jägersberg). In the meantime, most of the Groddeck archives have been moved to the Deutsches Literaturarchiv in Marbach, Germany.

[6] See the letter of 12th November 1922 from Groddeck to Ferenczi, in which he even expresses his deliberate desire not to understand.

[7] Could it even have been Sigmund Ferenczi who would later refer to his younger brother, Sándor, Melanie Klein, the wife of his colleague Arthur Klein (like Sigmund, a chemical engineer in a paper-mill)?

[8] Similarly the last letter from Sándor and Gizella Ferenczi to Professor Freud, on 4th May 1933, three weeks before Sándor's death:

Budapest, 4th May 1933

Dear Professor

Just a brief note to let you know that the date of your birthday is always present in our memory. We hope that the year to come will not bring any events as distressing as the previous year.

As for me, everything is much the same, my symptoms are unchanged. I try hard to have faith in the doctor's optimistic statements.

Your S. and G. Ferenczi

Gizella Ferenczi added a personal letter to these lines:

Dear Professor

From the few lines which Sándor has written to you from his bed, you see that he is still not what he was. I do not know what I can believe, what I can hope for! Levy hopes for an improvement soon – and I want *to believe him*. For the moment, my heart is full of grief. For your birthday – dear Professor – I wish that everything should go well for you.

Cordial greetings to your family,

Your faithful friend Fr. G.

[9] A certain number of people knew about these events, which took place over several years. We find an echo of them in the letters of Frédéric Kovács to Vilma Kovács (see Appendix 1 to this volume). The story is also evoked in the fine novel by D.M. Thomas, *The White Hotel*, published in 1981, first by Victor Gollancz, then by Penguin Books. The French translation was published by Albin Michel. The novel tells of the analysis and the history of one of Freud's patients: imaginary case or unpublished case.

[10] See 'The Principle of Relaxation and Neocatharsis', *Final Contributions to the Problems and Methods of Psychoanalysis*, pp.108-125.

Georg Groddeck

Groddeck's father, Karl Groddeck, a physician, was the son of a court councillor who had been Mayor of Danzig. Groddeck's mother, Karoline Koberstein, was the daughter of the German literary historian, August Koberstein, who had taught for many years at Schulpforta, where Klopstock, Lessing, Ranke and Nietzsche had been pupils.

1852 Groddeck's parents marry.

1853 Birth of Groddeck's brother Carl, who suffers from epilepsy.

1854 Birth of Hans.

1861 Birth of Wolf.

1864 Birth of Groddeck's sister Lina, who is frail and often ill.

1866 Birth of Georg on 13th October 1866 in Bad Kösen on the Saale. He is handed over to 'radiant Bertha', the wet nurse, and is dressed as a girl, up to the age of nine.

1878 At the age of 12 he becomes ill when he is due to return to Schulpforta, his boarding school. He becomes lazy and undisciplined, and is frequently beaten and locked up at school.

1881 Financial speculations ruin the Groddeck family. Groddeck's father joins a medical practice and Georg accompanies him on his house visits.

1885 Karl Groddeck dies of a heart attack, leaving his family in financial straits. Groddeck's older brother, Carl, gets an editorial job on the *Vossischen Zeitung*. Georg studies medicine under Bismarck's famous personal doctor, Ernst Schweninger, who teaches hydrotherapy, dietetics and massage. Groddeck becomes his devoted assistant.

1889 Groddeck qualifies as a doctor.

1892 Groddeck's mother dies whilst he is on military service.

1894 Meets Else von der Goltz (née Neumann), a divorcée with two children.

1896 Groddeck marries Else.

1900 Together with his sister Lina, Groddeck opens his own sanatorium – with fifteen beds – in Baden-Baden.

1901 Birth of his daughter Barbara, and separation from Else. Groddeck seeks solace in work and writing.

1904 Lina dies.

1906 Wolf dies. Groddeck becomes responsible for his deceased brother's wife and children.

1909 Publishes *Hin zu Gottnatur* [Towards God Nature]. Groddeck is exhausted and depressed. Meets his patient Fräulein G., who is so weak and ill that, in order to save her life, he has no choice but to show her the greatest warmth, friendship and empathy, indeed, to 'mother' her; he subsequently develops a new psychosomatic perspective and an appreciation of the significance of symbols. Groddeck's short novel, *The Vicar of Langewiesche*, a finely crafted study of morality and the individual's struggle with his conscience in an hostile and authoritarian environment, is published in the feuilleton section of the *Frankfurter Zeitung* in five instalments.

1910 Overcomes his depression fully.

1913 Publishes *Nasamecu*, a book of popular medicine. Groddeck's patients tell him about Freud. He reads *The Psychopathology of Everyday Life* and *The Interpretation of Dreams*, and is deeply impressed.

1914 First World War. His brother Hans dies. Groddeck runs a Red Cross hospital, but has qualms about healing soldiers only to send them back to the trenches, and is dismissed.

1915 Meets Emmy von Voigt, a young widow of Swedish descent, whom he treats and cures and who becomes his assistant. In order to acquaint his patients with his ideas, he gives regular Wednesday lectures and edits a house journal, *Satanarium*.

1917 Begins to relate his dreams to the assembled listeners. On May 27th Groddeck writes his first letter to Freud, who replies enthusiastically on 5th June, and mentions Ferenczi in the same letter. Publishes first psychosomatic works, including 'Psychic Conditioning and the Psychoanalytic Treatment of Organic Disorders'.

1918 Stekel edits Groddeck's first psychoanalytic novel *Thomas Weltlein*, which is later published as *The Seeker of Souls*.

1919 Sends manuscript of *The Seeker of Souls* to Freud, who recommends Groddeck to the Berlin Psychoanalytic Association.

1920 Meets Freud for the first time at the 6th International Psychoanalytic Congress in The Hague.

1921 Groddeck invites Freud to spend a few weeks in Baden-Baden. Ferenczi announces himself for August.

1923 Marries Emmy. Groddeck publishes *The Book of the It*, which is well received in analytical circles. Freud publishes *The Ego and the Id*, and Groddeck accuses him of borrowing his terminology. Freud, who has contracted cancer, for a time considers being treated and analysed by Groddeck.

1925 Groddeck visits Freud in Vienna before one of his operations. Writes *The Meaning of Illness*. 16th May: first number of *The Ark*, a fortnightly house journal, containing articles on the It and psychoanalysis, resistance, transference.

1926 Freud congratulates Groddeck on his 60th birthday. Further articles in *The Ark*: 'Psychoanalytic thoughts on arteriosclerosis'; 'On bisexuality'; 'Constipation as a form of resistance'; 'Psychoanalysis and organic diseases'. In the autumn he presents a series of lectures in Berlin on the It, including 'The It and the Gospels.'

1928 Lectures in England. 'Remarks on the embryonal time in relation to later life' read before a meeting of the British Psycho-Analytical Society.

1929 'Memoirs'.

1930 'Ernst Schweninger – the physician.' Invitation to attend the Congress for Sex Research in London, where he presents a paper on 'Organic disease specifically as an expression of sexuality.'

1932 'Vision, the world of the eye, and seeing without the eye.'

1933 'Man's stomach and its soul'; 'The mouth and its soul'; 'The influence of English literature in Germany'; 'The psychical conditioning of cancer.'

1934 Has heart attack in January. On the instigation of Frieda Fromm-Reichmann, the Swiss Psychoanalytic Association invites Groddeck to give a talk: 'Vision, the world of the eye, and seeing without the eye.' After the talk he suffers another heart attack.
On June 11th, Groddeck dies of heart failure in Medard Boss' Sanatorium Schloss Knonau, Switzerland.

List of Photographs and Illustrations

Nos: 1, 3, 6, 7, 8, courtesy of Judith Dupont.
Nos: 4, 5, courtesy of Beate Schuh, GEORG GRODDECK GESELLSCHAFT.
No. 2, courtesy of Dr. Herbert Will, Munich.

FRONT COVER: Sándor Ferenczi (top); Georg Groddeck (below).
(Courtesy of Judith Dupont and Beate Schuh respectively).

Photographs and Illustrations

1. Gizella and Sándor Ferenczi on holiday in Baden-Baden.

2. Groddeck's sanatorium, Villa Marienhöhe, viewed from the road.

3. Sándor Ferenczi on the veranda of Marienhöhe.

4. Georg and Emmy Groddeck in the garden, c. 1923.

5. Groddeck's hut. Georg, Emmy (with great-niece), and niece.

6. Elma Laurvik (née Pálos), Gizella Ferenczi's daughter.
Oil painting by Olga Székely-Kovács, c.1924.

7. Gizella and Sándor Ferenczi with Elizabeth Severn in Spain, October 1928.

8. Sándor Ferenczi's 55th Birthday Party in Budapest.

Along righthand wall: Frédéric Kovács (2nd up from right); Gizella (3rd); Sándor (4th); István Hollós (6th); Imre Hermann (8th); Alice Bálint (9th). Along curtain at back: 2nd from left Michael Bálint (with glasses); 3rd: Alice Hermann. Opposite Bálint – Vilma Kovács (looking to her right). Top left corner, 3rd down from curtain: Dr. Lajos Lévy. Opposite Lévy – Mme. Róheim.

THE LETTERS

Sándor Ferenczi to Georg Groddeck

MAGYARORSZÁGI
PSZICHOANALITIKAI EGYESÜLET
(FREUD-TÁRSASÁG)[1]

Budapest, 26th April 1921

To Dr. Georg Groddeck
Baden-Baden

———————————

Miss Ivonne von Szabó,[2] aged seventeen, has for two years been
suffering from spastic paresis[3] of the lower extremities[4] (a consequence of a cerebral complication following Spanish flu[5] –
although she can walk briskly), and from a proneness to catatonic[6] muscular spasms as well as occasional violent trembling.
Of late she also has a compulsion to tear everything up. Psychologically she is very receptive. In my opinion she requires a
combination of physical and psychological treatment, to which
end I have recommended your institution to her family.

Yours faithfully,

Dr. S. Ferenczi

[1] Letterhead: Hungarian Psychoanalytic Association (Freud-Society).
[2] Apparently a patient of Ferenczi's.
[3] Spastic – the inability to relax specific muscles, which inhibits normal muscle action;
paresis – partial paralysis or weakness of muscle.
[4] The legs.
[5] After the First World War (1918-19) the so-called 'Spanish flu' broke out world-
wide. It is estimated that some twenty million people died in Europe alone. Those
who survived the initial infection were sometimes left with aftereffects. While not
proven, Parkinson's disease in later life has been linked to this influenza.
[6] Catatonic – intermittent uncontrolled muscle contractions.

Sándor Ferenczi to Georg Groddeck

Garmisch-Partenkirchen[1]
Kurheim Wigger[2]
17th August 1921

Dear Colleague,[3]

I am at present taking a break at the above sanatorium and am to meet up with Professor Freud around mid-September, somewhere in Germany.[4] Hence I am confronted by the question of where to spend the first two weeks of September (possibly even from 27th/28th August onwards). I thus had the idea of combining work with pleasure and would like to ask you whether you could reserve for us (my wife[5] and myself) appropriate accommodation in your sanatorium. If this is possible, then please let me know your normal rates for board and lodging.

What determined me in choosing this holiday venue was above all the hope of being able to study, with your permission, and at close quarters, how you apply psychoanalysis in the treatment of organic diseases – something that interests me enormously.

I take this opportunity to congratulate you sincerely on your *Seeker of Souls* which I am reviewing in the next issue of *Imago*.[6]

By the way, I hear from Professor Freud that we can shortly expect something very special and interesting from you again.[7]

Hoping for a speedy reply, if possible by return of post, and with best wishes,

Yours sincerely,

S. Ferenczi

[1] Garmisch-Partenkirchen, a town in the Bavarian Alps, Germany.

[2] The Kurheim was part of the 'Sanatorium Wigger', founded by Dr. Wigger, and served the less seriously ill or those seeking rest and only slight medical supervision.

[3] The German form of address is extremely formal and impersonal, literally, 'Very honoured Mr. Colleague', and is to this day used in all business communications.

[4] This meeting of the 'Secret Committee', which was formed in 1912 with the express purpose of preserving the spirit of Freud's teaching, was held in Hildesheim (see card from the Commitee, 23rd September 1921, p.7).

[5] Gizella Ferenczi (1865-1949), née Altschul; 'Pálos' by first marriage.

[6] Groddeck's *Der Seelensucher* (which can also be translated as 'The Searcher for Souls') was the first psychoanalytic novel. Ferenczi's review appeared in German in *Imago* (1921), 7, pp.356ff., and in English in Sándor Ferenczi: *Final Contributions to the Problems and Methods of Psycho-Analysis* pp.344-348.

[7] A reference to Groddeck's most famous book, *The Book of the It* (Vision Press, London, 1950, reprinted Vintage, New York, 1961), originally published as *Das Buch vom Es* in 1923 by the Internationaler Psychoanalytischer Verlag (Vienna/Leipzig). The book is in the form of letters, written to a woman friend – his future wife, Emmy – and signed as 'Patrik Troll'. Groddeck's childhood nickname was 'Pat', and his affectionate name for his wife was 'Troll', after the trolls and Peer Gynt's association with them in Ibsen's *Peer Gynt* (1867), a play Groddeck loved.

Sándor Ferenczi to Georg Groddeck

G. Partenkirchen, 24th August 1921

Kurheim Wigger

Dear Colleague,

After some prevarication I decided simply to accept your kind invitation.[1] Latest plans suggest we won't be arriving before Sept 5th.[2] Meanwhile we hope to meet up a few times with Professor Freud, who happens to be staying in the immediate vicinity (Seefeld/Tyrol).[3] I will let you know in good time the exact date of our arrival.

With kind regards, also from my wife,

Yours sincerely,

S. Ferenczi

[1] Most of Groddeck's letters have not survived, including the one he must have sent between Ferenczi's letters of 17th and 24th August. Only three of Groddeck's letters to Ferenczi, and one to Gizella, have been preserved. Gizella Ferenczi wrote to Margaretha Honegger, Groddeck's literary executor, that Ferenczi destroyed letters, once read, as a matter of course. However, because of their highly personal nature, it is very probable that Ferenczi destroyed Groddeck's letters intentionally. Furthermore, it wouldn't be unreasonable to speculate that, given the very personal content of these letters, Gizella herself may have been less than enthusiastic about their preservation.
[2] In fact, Sándor and Gizella Ferenczi signed the guestbook on 8th September and stayed until 17th September. The entry reads: 'Dr. Sándor Ferenczi & Frau Gisela Ferenczi' 8/17 Sept. Address: Budapest VII Nagydiófa u.3.
[3] Like most bourgeois Viennese, Freud spent holidays in the country. He had a long history of visiting the Tyrol region of northern Italy.

Sándor Ferenczi to Georg Groddeck

MAGYARORSZÁGI
PSZICHOANALITIKAI EGYESÜLET
(FREUD-TÁRSASÁG)

Dear Doctor Groddeck![1]

I cannot leave without thanking you again, or – if you will allow me to put it thus – telling you what warm feelings of friendship I have for you!

Until we meet again!

Ferenczi

[1] Although undated, Ferenczi's salutation and letterhead suggest that this note be placed here. He is presumably still in Baden-Baden.

6

[Card from the 'Committee' to Georg Groddeck][1]

Hildesheim, 23rd September 1921

Hope you were pleased with [my] substitute.[2] *Freud*

      Were you? *Ferenczi*

Best regards, *Dr. Rank*

ditto *Abraham*   *Ernest Jones*

      Hanns Sachs   *Eitingon*

---

[1] This card to Groddeck is signed by the seven members of the 'Secret Committee' (see p.17, n. 21), and was first published in the Freud-Groddeck correspondence included in *The Meaning of Illness: Selected Psychoanalytic Writings* by Georg Groddeck, with an introduction by Lore Schacht, Ed. (Hogarth Press, London, 1977, reprinted Karnac, London, 1988).

[2] Freud is referring to Ferenczi's recent visit to Groddeck's sanatorium just prior to the Committee meeting.

Sándor Ferenczi to Georg Groddeck

Budapest, Christmas Day 1921

I.   Dear Friend,[1]

    I have to admit that before I felt able to address you this openly I had to overcome a certain resistance – indeed quite a powerful one. For a very, very long time now, I have taken pleasure in maintaining an aloof reticence, and I like to cover up my feelings, often even with close friends. I don't have to explain to you that this represents a regression to the infantile. Did I want too much attention, or was my mother – the mother of 11 surviving children,[2]

7

of which I was the 8th – too strict? As I remember it, I certainly didn't get enough love, and did get too much severity from her as a child.[3] Being sentimental, hugging and cuddling simply never happened in our family. On the contrary, deferential respect was what we practised in the presence of our parents, etc. How could anything but hypocrisy result from such an upbringing? Preserving appearances, concealing everything 'unmentionable' was all important. That's how I became an outstanding pupil at school whilst masturbating in secret;[4] simulating modesty, never so much as an obscene word – whilst visiting prostitutes, with stolen money, on the quiet. Now and again I would make tentative attempts to show what I was really like. I thus once 'accidentally' let my mother get hold of a list containing all the obscene words I could think of. Instead of being told the facts of life and offered help, I got a moral lecture.[5]

It is then, even objectively speaking, amazing in view of these antecedents that I can declare myself totally vanquished by your unpretentious manner, your natural kindness and friendliness. I have never been so open with another man, not even with 'Siegmund' (Freud), whose name caused me to misspell the word vanquished [besi(e)gt].[6] Now and again I would let him analyse me[7] (once for 3, once for 4-5 weeks),[8] – we went on holiday together every summer,[9] for years: I could never be completely free and open with him; I felt that he expected too much of this 'deferential respect' from me; he was too big for me, there was too much of the father. As a result, on our very first working evening together in Palermo,[10] when he wanted to work with me on the famous paranoia text (Schreber),[11] and started to dictate something, I jumped up in a sudden rebellious outburst, exclaiming that this was no working together, dictating to me. 'So this is what you are like?' he said, taken aback. 'You obviously want to do the whole thing yourself.' That said, he now spent every evening working on his own, I was left out in the cold – bitter feelings constricted my throat. (Of course I now know what this 'working alone in the evenings' and this 'constriction of the throat' signifies: I wanted, of course, to be loved by Freud.)[12]

If I was as talented a writer as you I would continue in this vein and discharge my physical and mental pain on paper. (N.B: I wasn't being quite honest then! I do think I am a talented writer; I remember how hurt I was when someone made derogatory comments about something I had written, and, when I was younger, about a poem.)[13]

II.   Anyway, for the moment I will defer regaling you with the story of my development 'ab ovo'.[14] Let's continue with the here and now. So:

Your letter came at a critical moment, after one of those many, many awful nights, when I woke up barely able to breathe, with cold, clammy skin, pains around the heart, virtually no pulse, (though occasional palpitations), despairing of the future and Groddeck,[15] and thinking I was staring death in the face. Your letter spurred me on to greater efforts; it helped me remove my mask in front of my wife, too – albeit partially. I spoke to her again about my sexual frustration, about my suppressed love for her daughter[16] (who should have been my wife; indeed who was in effect my bride until a somewhat disparaging remark of Freud's prompted me to fight this love tooth and nail – literally to push the girl away from me).[17]

Oddly enough, with us these confessions usually end with me

drawing closer to her again – overwhelmed by her goodness and forgiving nature. Whether it was this, or the result of taking hot baths again, since then the nightly drop in my body temperature is a little less deathlike than before. I'm also avidly doing my gymnastic exercises and the stomach-treading again (up to 40!).[18] But I'm far from feeling well yet.

I will list the symptoms for you:

The first thing that comes to mind is my inhibition about work. (Association of ideas: You mustn't outshine father.) In 1915/16 when I was garrisoned (for eighteen months) in a small Hungarian town,[19] and had time on my hands I devised a great, indeed a 'grand' theory that genital development evolved as a reaction on the part of animals to the threat of dehydration whilst adapting to life on land. Not once could I get myself to write down this valuable theory – my best to date. The relevant data lie dozing in my writing-desk, scattered about all over the place.[20] I'm happy enough to 'talk' about the theory; once – actually twice – I explained it all to Freud, Rank, Jones, Abraham, etc.,[21] most recently in Hildesheim.[22] But 'write' about it, and I get backache, due, of course, to my aorta, which, according to the X-ray, is enlarged. A few weeks ago I developed arthritic swellings in my right wrist, which, of course, again kept me from writing. The wrist now feels free again.

At the same time (no – it was still in 1914, in Munich)[23] I developed my philosophical views in front of Lou Salomé,[24] which more or less correspond to those in 'Beyond',[25] although they end up somewhat differently. I also spoke to Freud[26] about these views on occasion. But try and write them down, and I hadn't the courage to do it. Time and again I've let myself be drawn into writing small *ad hoc* pieces instead of this quintessential work, to keep people from quite forgetting me.

The American doctors[27] who are at present studying with Freud have invited me to give two lectures in Vienna on meta-psychology. I have accepted; and am to speak on 6th January. Not a word written or prepared as yet.

III.   What often comes to mind when I consider this symptom (inhibition about work) is: it just isn't worth it, i.e: there is nothing I could get from this world that would warrant my 'offerings' to it. Anal eroticism, presumably: I won't 'release' anything till I get a present. But what this present might be? It can only be the child my wife ought to give me, – or, conversely, the 'child' which I would like to bear and give to the world (father and mother).

The trouble with this is, my eroticism refuses to be satisfied by barren explanations. I, my 'It', isn't interested in analytical interpretations, but wants something real, a young wife, a child![28]

(By the way, wouldn't you agree that the famous saying about 'screaming for a child' is simply the inversion of yearning to hear children shrieking?)

I notice that I'm imitating your 'Letters to a Woman Friend'[29] in peppering this letter with these entertaining morsels. Are you by any chance this female friend for me, or am I using your friendship in a homosexual way to replace her? –

Perhaps I should get on with telling you about the dream I had last night – not easy to write about, since it was an entirely 'Hungarian' dream:

So there I am in the dream happily singing a Hungarian folk-song, of which I particularly remember two verses on waking up.

They go like this more or less (roughly translated):

"This is what the old Jew tells me,
'Here! – it's from my market stall.'
'I want nothing from your stall,
I don't want you, old Jew, either.'"

"This is what Fáy Gyula tells me (name of a dashing man),
'I'll buy you, dearest, dresses, ribbons',
'Don't need your dresses, ribbons, Fáy,
All I want is you.'"

(Translated literally:

"Furthermore the old Jew tells me,
'I will give you rouge and make-up',
'Have no need of rouge or make-up,
I don't want you, old Jew, either.'

Furthermore Fáy Gyula tells me,
'Would you like some linen, dresses?'
'Have no need of fabrics, dresses,
All I want is Fáy himself.')

What comes to mind about this, is:

Yesterday evening, Christmas Eve, just *en famille*,[30] I did eat 'rather too much'. I've often remarked how ridiculous it is to have such elaborate meals when we're on our own. Occasionally I looked across to the kitchen, where our two servant-girls were singing and enjoying themselves with their friends. The two girls are sisters. The younger one is 16, extremely nice, an innocent country lass whom we've only recently taken on. She has remarkably red lips (wears make-up; the lips, though, are naturally red).

12

IV.   The older one, the cook, is barely 19-20 years old herself. She has, as I was able to establish during the course of a medical examination, remarkably firm, ripe breasts, with enormous nipples which became erect during the examination.

Interpretation: these pretty girls didn't want an old Jew like me![31] N.B: I was telling a friend yesterday who, although older than me, still has black hair: 'Your vitality is amazing. Look how old and grey I am.' I must have grown old, I thought to myself, in order to be like my wife, who is older than me.[32] My friend's wife is a fresh young blonde.

I picked up that folksong as a child from the peasant women working in our vineyard.[33] I also heard father and mother sing the song; they too got it from those women. I often yearned for the earthy charms of those peasant girls in that vineyard; indeed, I resorted to 'amor ancillaris'[34] a lot. I had to go to the vineyard with my suppressed passions.

I was lying on my left side when I awoke, and my heart – as a result of being compressed – was pounding.[35] I couldn't get back to sleep again.

Addendum: that song was somehow 'bisexual' in the dream. It seemed to me that the said 'Fáy Gyula' was at one and the same time also some beautiful <u>Lady</u> Fáy.

'Fáy' is a surname. But the word 'Fáj' = 'it hurts'.[36] Whether my heart actually hurt me – physically or emotionally – I do not know.

Addendum 2: Yesterday I had occasional pangs of conscience for having felt so jolly, despite hearing of a (good-for-nothing) nephew's suicide only the day before. He very much wanted to become a doctor, even a psychoanalyst, which, however, I sought to prevent – knowing about his flawed character. Was I, too, responsible for his death? I could ask myself.

You are most probably right in surmising that at least part of my fear of dying is due to wishing my wife dead. In a dream recently I was applying myself to giving medical treatment to a deep headwound on her temple.

So clearly I don't want to hurt her, and tell her nothing, or too little, about my treacherous thoughts; – but instead hurt myself with pains in the heart.

I've told you enough about myself now! I'm aware of course that it's usual to tell one's wife everything. Have to admit, though, to feeling very embarrassed about your wife knowing. As I've said, it wasn't easy for me, either, to put aside my pride in being an academic, and to present myself not as being above it all and as your competitor, but as naive and childlike – 'humble'[37] is the word that comes to mind.

Make of this letter, then, what you will!

In friendship,

Yours sincerely,

Ferenczi

Please forward the enclosed feuilleton to Dr. M. Eitingon, Berlin/W, Rauchstrasse 4, as soon as possible.

Addendum 3. Out of a sense of duty I felt compelled to show this letter to my wife. I will thus use this opportunity to add a third postscript, because I want to tell you what an important role my ultra-susceptibility to cold plays in my life. While I was writing this letter to you it was a little colder than usual in the room (even though the weather wasn't cold outside: 4-5 degrees Réaumur above zero.) By the time I had finished the letter I was quite cold, my pulse quickened; back- and headaches were much worse, probably due to the lack of blood in my skin and the enormous increase of tension. I've often thought that I revert at night to the poikilothermy of fish;[38] and am sure that all human beings do this at times – which is why they need to keep warm at night. But in my case, I completely stop generating warmth, even when wrapped in 2-3 woollen blankets, probably due to my inhibited breathing.[39] Am I trying to behave like a fish, or to enact my genital theory of fishes which I won't write down? Am I undergoing a latent uraemia? I don't know. Walking warms me up quickly, even when it's very cold.

My wife sends you her fond regards.

---

[1] First letter with an informal salutation.

[2] Rosa Ferenczi (1840-1921), née Eibenschütz, gave birth to 12 children. However, the tenth, a daughter named Vilma Ferenczi, died in the year she was born (1878) from diphtheria. Ferenczi actually uses the phrase '11 living children', which confirms Judith Dupont's comment that Ferenczi, who was almost five years old at the time, did not forget this sister. In fact, Ferenczi mentions his guilt as a child at the death of Vilma (uncovered through his mutual analysis) in *The Clinical Diary of Sándor Ferenczi*, ed. Judith Dupont (Cambridge, MA, and London: Harvard University Press, 1988, p.121).

[3] For more on Ferenczi's view of his treatment by his mother see his *Clinical Diary*, pp.45, 86, 99.

[4] In a 19th January 1932 entry in the *Clinical Diary* (p.15), Ferenczi writes: '[I] compensated in [my] youth by endless masturbatory activity, the peculiarity of which can be gauged by the ejaculation up to the sky [Ejaculatio usque ad coelum].' Cf. pp. 89, 134. In his 1919 paper, 'Technical difficulties in the analysis of a case of hysteria' (Ferenczi, *Further Contributions*, p.205), Ferenczi writes of a patient who, in exhibiting 'onania perpetua (incompleta)', reminds him of his own case.

[5] Ferenczi briefly refers to this event in his 1911 paper 'On obscene words', in *First Contributions to Psycho-Analysis* (Karnac, reprinted 1994, pp.132-153).

[6] Ferenczi misspelled 'besigt' – leaving out the second 'e'. However, he caught his mistake and, as can be seen from the original handwritten letter, he then inserted the missing 'e'. Earlier editors (French/German editions), who did not have the handwritten original letter available, have erroneously cited Ferenczi as having made a mistake about which word he misspelled – that he misspelled 'Siegmund', not 'besiegt'. However, Ferenczi was clear on which word he'd got wrong, so that his conscious

spelling of 'Sigmund' as 'Siegmund' (Freud) was, as Ferenczi often did in his letters, a clever play on words, i.e. 'Siegmund': lit: 'Sieg' – victory, and 'Mund' – mouth, suggesting verbal conquest/verbal victory. Also, there is the intriguing parallel component of 'Sieg' in both words: 'Siegmund' and 'besiegt', and of his intentionally misspelling the first, and unconsciously misspelling the second – 'besi͜egt' – which is the correct spelling of the initial syllable in the name 'Sigmund'.

[7] Ferenczi's passive language belies what we know to have been Ferenczi's most determined pursuit of Freud for analysis. See *Freud-Ferenczi Correspondence*, Vol. II, pp.xxi-xxvii, and J. Dupont, 'Freud's analysis of Ferenczi as revealed by their correspondence', *International Journal of Psycho-Analysis*, 75, [1994], pp.301-320.

[8] There were three periods of analysis: a few weeks in October 1914 (interrupted by Ferenczi's military service); three more weeks from 14th June to 5th July 1916; and, finally, from 29th September until 9th October 1916.

[9] The first of these trips was in 1908, only months after they met, when Ferenczi accompanied Freud and his family on a holiday to Berchtesgaden, Germany – a regular holiday resort for the Freuds – near the Austrian border and just south of Salzburg.

[10] In 1910, Freud and Ferenczi travelled from Leyden, Netherlands, to Palermo, Sicily, via Paris, Florence, Rome and Naples ((31st August-26th September).

[11] Freud, 'Psycho-Analytic Notes Upon an Autobiographical Account of a Case of Paranoia (Dementia Paranoides),' Standard Edition (1911), 12, pp.3-82.

[12] This incident in Palermo was the first open disagreement between Freud and Ferenczi.

[13] In a statement solicited by Michael Balint, Zsofia Ferenczi, nicknamed Zsuka, Sándor's youngest sister and the last of the 12 Ferenczi children, said: 'When he [Sándor] was 24 years old, he wrote the following poem for my mother:

An der Schwelle neuen Lebens	On the threshold of new life
grüsse ich Dich, Mutter meine.	I greet you, mother mine.
Niemand anders, Du alleine,	No one else, you alone,
Du verstehst mich, wenn ich weine.	will understand me, when I weep.
Und ich weine heute innig	And today I'm sorely weeping
heisse Tränen, heisse Wahre.	burning tears, burnt offerings.
Hingestreckt sind in der Bahre	Borne to you on this bier
Vierundzwanzig meiner Jahre!	are these my twenty-four years!

I can't remember any more. But he often wrote to my mother from Vienna lovely poems reminiscent of Heine.' Heinrich Heine (1797-1856), German Jewish lyric poet and one of the greatest writers in the German language, is perhaps best known for his *Buch der Lieder* (1827), made up of sublime dream and love poetry.

[14] Phrase in Latin – 'ab ovo' (from the egg) – in original. Ferenczi appears to confirm his desire to initiate a kind of analysis with Groddeck. This desire is realised and soon turns into a form of mutual analysis, as in the next year, 1922, Ferenczi was again treated by Groddeck at his sanatorium, and on this visit also analysed Groddeck for about six or seven sessions (see Groddeck to Freud, 31st May 1923, *The Meaning of Illness*).

[15] Earlier in September, at his Baden-Baden sanatorium, Groddeck, as Ferenczi's physician, had some success in alleviating Ferenczi's chronic symptoms. Groddeck's treatments included hot baths, personal massage and vigorous pounding, special diets,

fasting and reduced intake of liquids, breathing and physical exercises. Groddeck frequently inspired great confidence in his patients and admirers. Given the nature of his unorthodox regimen – often physically painful – his patients would have to trust him to submit to it.

[16] Elma Pálos (1887-1972), whose married name was 'Laurvik'.

[17] Ferenczi had a complex triangular relationship with Gizella and her daughter Elma. This episode is extensively recounted in the Ferenczi literature and is a recurring theme in *The Freud-Ferenczi Correspondence,* Vol. I, (1993). See A. Haynal's Introduction to Vol. I, p.xxiif. for the background on the relationship. For the pivotal role played by Freud, see A. Haynal and E. Falzeder, 'Healing through love? A unique dialogue in the history of psychoanalysis,' *Free Associations,* Part I, 2 (21), pp.1-20; also, Dupont (1995).

[18] stomach-treading – 'Bauchtreten': one of Groddeck's treatment exercises.

[19] Pápa, 130 km. south-west of Budapest. In October 1914, Ferenczi was conscripted and posted to Pápa as chief medical officer in the Hungarian Hussars until spring 1916.

[20] In fact, Ferenczi published this work in Vienna in 1924, as *Versuch einer Genitaltheorie* (Internationaler Psychoanalytischer Verlag; in English: *Thalassa: A Theory of Genitality,* New York: *Psychoanalytic Quarterly,* 1938, reprinted London: Karnac, 1989). In *Thalassa,* Ferenczi expounds an almost cosmic theory, that 'the whole of life is determined by a tendency to return to the womb', equating the process of birth with the phylogenetic transition of animal life from water to land, and linking coitus to the idea of 'thalassal regression: the longing for the sea-life from which man emerged in primeval times'. It is noteworthy that *Thalassa* has probably become the best known of Ferenczi's works, and is widely cited, often in non-psychoanalytic literature.

[21] Otto Rank (1884-1939), Ernest Jones (1879-1958), and Karl Abraham (1877-1925), members of Freud's inner circle. Along with Ferenczi and Hanns Sachs (1881-1947), they comprised Freud's 'Secret Committee', which began its work in Vienna in May 1913. Max Eitingon (1881-1943) became a member in 1919. See Phyllis Grosskurth's *The Secret Ring: Freud's Inner Circle and the Politics of Psychoanalysis* (Reading, Mass: Addison-Wesley, 1991), for a recent treatment of the 'Committee'.

[22] Ferenczi first presented his ideas on this genital theory to the 'Committee' in 1919.

[23] Ferenczi is probably referring to the 4th Congress of the International Psycho-Analytical Association held in Munich in September 1913.

[24] Lou Andreas-Salomé (1861-1937), German-Russian psychoanalyst and writer perhaps best known for her famous friendships with Nietzsche and Rilke, came to Freud and psychoanalysis in 1911. In 1913, Salomé writes of her conversations with Ferenczi in her journal (pp.170-172, *The Freud Journal,* London: Quartet Books, 1987). Salomé, who held Freud's affection and admiration, respected both Ferenczi and Groddeck. As early as 1913 Salomé sensed Ferenczi's place in relation to Freud: 'I am passionately interested in [Ferenczi's] work and in his method of working. Perhaps publication of Ferenczi's ideas is premature with respect to Freud's present and next endeavours, but they really are complementary. So Ferenczi's time must come', *The Freud Journal,* (p.137).

[25] 'Beyond' – 'Jenseits': a reference to Freud's book *Beyond the Pleasure Principle* [*Jenseits des Lustprinzips*], 1920.

[26] 'Auch Freud' was misread as 'Anna Freud' in the original French and German

17

editions. However, as a matter of interest, in their long-standing relationship, Freud's daughter, Anna (1895-1982), held a great deal of respect for Ferenczi and this included his later controversial technical innovations (*Freud-Ferenczi Correspondence*, Vol. III). Also, it is not well known, but Anna is said to have participated with her father and Ferenczi in their early experiments in thought transference (G. Hidas, 'Flowing-Over Transference, Countertransference, Telepathy: Subjective Dimensions of the Psychoanalytic Relationship in Ferenczi's Thinking,' in Aron and Harris, 1993, p.209).

[27] In 1921, the American members of the New York Psychoanalytic Society were Abram Kardiner, MD (1891-1981), Leonard Blumgart, MD (1880-1951), Clarence Oberndorf, MD (1882-1954), Monroe A. Meyer, MD (1892-1939) and Albert Polon, MD (1882-1926). In those days, it was customary for Americans, particularly New Yorkers, interested in becoming analysts to travel to Vienna to have an analysis, usually with Freud. See Kardiner, *My Analysis With Freud: Reminiscences* (Norton, 1977), and Oberndorf, *A History of Psychoanalysis in America* (Grune & Stratton, 1953).

[28] Ferenczi expresses frustration that having chosen to marry Gizella, an older woman beyond child-bearing age, instead of the younger Elma, he lost his chance to father a child. He is left only with the opportunity to 'father' (or 'mother') psychoanalytical insights. To some degree, Ferenczi held Freud responsible for his situation (see p.19).

[29] Groddeck's *The Book of the It* [*Das Buch vom Es*]. See p.5, n.7.

[30] Sándor and Gizella Ferenczi, and her daughters Elma and Magda Pálos. Magda married Ferenczi's youngest brother, Lajos, and was Gizella's youngest daughter by her first marriage to Géza Pálos.

[31] Another interpretation of the dream suggests that the 'old Jew' in the dream represents Freud. (Personal communication to the editor from Eva Brabant).

[32] Gizella was eight years older than Sándor.

[33] Ferenczi grew up in Miskolcz, a provincial town 150 km. north-east of Budapest. The Ferenczis owned vineyards on the outskirts of the town.

[34] Latin in original. Lit: 'maid-servant love'. In his *Clinical Diary*, Ferenczi recounts his memories of early sexual traumas at the hands of a nurse, and a housemaid, when he was six years old.

[35] Medically, sleeping on the left side would not make one's heart pound.

[36] Ferenczi's raising of 'it hurts' in this context could be seen as prefiguring his later interest in real trauma (E. Brabant, personal communication).

[37] 'Humble' in English in original.

[38] Another allusion to *Thalassa* and his theory that certain human behaviour reflects a propensity to regress to an earlier evolutionary developmental stage. See also 'The unwelcome child and his death instinct' for Ferenczi's note on his own case: 'In one special case there was even a quite peculiar, intense cooling down at night, with subnormal temperatures, difficult to explain organically' (Ferenczi,1929, p.104).

[39] The clinical state which arises from renal failure: i.e. an excess of waste-products (urea) in the blood. Some of Ferenczi's symptoms – headache, insomnia, and breathing problems – correspond to aspects of a clinical diagnosis of uraemia.

Sándor Ferenczi to Georg Groddeck

Budapest, 27th February 1922

Dear Groddeck,[1]

How to begin? We've been out of touch (my fault) for so long. My original letter,[2] your reply which I reread today: all past history now. I think it's best to start from scratch again.

There has been a marked improvement in my condition since early January. My visit to Vienna,[3] where I gave two lectures to Americans and Englishmen,[4] was still marred by ill health, but then, quite suddenly, my spirits lifted and my physical state improved remarkably. I cannot give you an exact explanation for this. Prof. Freud considered my overall physical symptoms for one to two hours; he persists in his original view that the crux of the matter is my hatred for <u>him</u>, because he stopped me (just like her father[5] did before him) from marrying the younger woman (now my stepdaughter). Hence my murderous intentions towards him[6] which express themselves in nightly death scenes (drop in body temperature; gasping for breath). These symptoms are, furthermore, overdetermined by my memories of watching my parents having intercourse.[7] I must admit it did me good to talk for once to this dearly loved father[8] about my hate feelings.

That my heart condition has improved is probably also due to the methodically applied 'stomach treading' which my wife carries out on me twice daily. We (my wife and I) are making a lot of propaganda in Budapest about this 'ordeal', as well as about your 'Nasamecu.'[9] I have already persuaded a few people to order your

19

book[10] from Hirzel.[11] Fact is, I can now get up the steep hill in Budapest of some 100 metres in quarter of an hour without getting out of breath. For the moment I'm not getting this drop in body temperature at night; on the other hand I've been swathed in wool since the onset of the cold season (the babe in swaddling clothes).[12] I'm ashamed to admit that (1) I am still taking a quarter of a Medinal pastille[13] every night; (2) am keeping my nostrils open with wire; and (3) am blocking my ears with cotton wool so that I can sleep. I can lay claim to a new symptom, namely <u>spots in front of my eyes</u>, which, however, I find I can alleviate through resting my head at a low angle. My own personally devised method for observing the inside of my eye has enabled me to discover not only an opacity in the *corpus vitreum* but also small scotomata in the *fovea centralis*, which I, of course, have surmised comes from the kidneys.[14]

I am better able to work intellectually now. I have completed the study on paralysis, which will be published shortly.[15] But I still haven't got down to the big historical-evolutionary treatise.[16]

I would, however, like to take up a few points in your last letter.[17] You ask: 'Who is at the receiving end of this coldness, this drop in body temperature; is the coldness directed towards someone else or to yourself, to your own sensuality?'[18] When I think about it I have to concede that it is probably a bit of both: denial of one's own libido generally because of feeling cold towards someone else, a woman. Recently my attentions have been engaged by the business of getting old, which actually gives me 'the creeps'.[19]

You were right in thinking that there was something of deeper significance about the town where I was garrisoned. The place was called <u>Pápa</u> (Pope); it was there that I felt uninterruptedly secure in the paternal womb.[20]

Well, I won't continue analysing it now; but will remember to torment you with it when we next meet.[21]

How I would love to come now (as also would my wife) in the spring. Unfortunately it is not permissible to grant oneself additional holidays unless one is feeling ill. We won't let anything prevent us, though, from spending the next summer holiday in Baden-Baden. But what is the climate like there in the glorious month of August?[22] Whatever the case, an underheated person like myself shouldn't be put off by even the hottest weather.[23]

From Baden-Baden we could go together to the Congress in Berlin.[24] It will be anything but dull there, I guarantee. India, Peru and France are represented for the first time.[25]

It all sounds wonderful and full of promise.

Please prepare something special for the Congress: let us say, about your experiences with psychoanalysis in treating heart and lung diseases. Your theory that psychological motivations underlie organic failure[26] will make a big impression.[27]

You will have left the isolated 'Haus Zink'[28] by now and be back in the beautiful Villa Marienhöhe.[29] Our thoughts follow you there all the time. We, my wife and I, can hardly believe that we spent barely ten days with you. We feel as if we had known you intimately for years, so vivid is the impression our stay made on us then and continues to make. The enormous kindness you and Frau von Voigt[30] showed us grows with the passage of time.

No – these things cannot be expressed in writing. We will have to come and sit on the lovely veranda again, and chat together on our own.

I will stop at this point, and close with fondest greetings to you, both from my wife and myself.

Let us hear from you <u>soon</u>!

Yours,

Ferenczi

[1] First letter using this salutation.

[2] Presumably the Christmas 1921 letter, see above, pp.7-15.

[3] First week of January (Jones, 1957, p.87).

[4] Ferenczi delivered a lecture on 6th January.

[5] Elma's father, Géza Pálos.

[6] There are echoes of this characterisation of Ferenczi as 'homicidal' by Jones (1957) in his Freud biography, pp.188-191.

[7] Classical Freudian concept of the traumatic significance of witnessing the 'primal scene' of parental intercourse.

[8] See 1932 *Clinical Diary* for Ferenczi's views of Freud as father figure (pp.184-185).

[9] 'Nasamecu' (from NAtura SAnat, MEdicus CUrat = nature heals, the doctor cures).

[10] *Nasamecu: Der gesunde und kranke Mensch* (The healthy and sick person), published in Leipzig, 1913, 'marks the transition between two phases in Groddeck's life, the phase during which he was Schweninger's pupil, and the phase during which he tried to be Freud's pupil. The book is written, on the one hand, in homage to his teacher Schweninger, whose therapeutic principles are commemorated in the title... It contains, on the other hand, a criticism of psychoanalysis which Groddeck at the time knew by hearsay only' (*The Meaning of Illness*, 1977, p.4). *Nasamecu* has chapters on bones, joints, muscles, nerves, nutrition, breathing, the circulation, etc.

[11] S. Hirzel, publisher in Leipzig. Hirzel was Groddeck's publisher, and his patient in Baden-Baden.

[12] Another of Ferenczi's many references to the 'child' = 'wise baby,' 'unwelcome child,' etc. Ferenczi was often referred to as the *'enfant terrible* of psychoanalysis' ('Child analysis in the analyses of adults' [1931], S. Ferenczi: *Final Contributions to the Problems and Methods of Psycho-Analysis*, p.127).

[13] A sleeping pill.

[14] Ferenczi had a kidney ailment, referred to by Gizella in her letter to Groddeck (28th February 1934) on p.115. Also referred to in a letter of Dr. W. Inman,Groddeck's patient and Ferenczi's analysand: 'In or about 1921 Ferenczi had been dangerously ill with nephritis. The physicians could do no more for him, so he packed off to Groddeck...' (Grossman, C. and Grossman, S., *The Wild Analyst*, 1965, p.155). Ferenczi was referred to Groddeck for nephrosclerosis.

[15] 'Psycho-analysis and the mental disorders of general paralysis of the insane' (1922), *Final Contributions to the Problems and Methods of Psychoanalysis*, pp.351-370. Originally published in German as a chapter of a book jointly written with István

22

Hollós in 1922; in English: *Psychoanalysis and the Psychic Disorder of General Paresis* (New York: Nervous and Mental Disease Publication Company, 1925).

[16] *Thalassa: A Theory of Genitality.*

[17] Letter not preserved.

[18] This question clearly reflects Groddeck's attempt to bring a psychological perspective to the analysis and treatment of Ferenczi's physical symptoms.

[19] Ferenczi was in his 49th year when he wrote this.

[20] 'Paternal womb' − 'Vaterleib': an allusion to the word 'Mutterleib' − 'womb', although it is also a play on the word 'Pápa'. Ferenczi's analysis with Freud had been interrupted by his move to Pápa. Freud visited him there, and they did some analysis.

[21] Ferenczi and Groddeck were involved in a form of mutual analysis. See Will, H: 'Ferenczi und Groddeck. Eine Freundschaft' (*Psyche* XLVIII, 8, pp.720-737, 1994).

[22] 'in the glorious month of August' − 'im wunderschönen Monat August' − is an allusion to Heinrich Heine's poem 'Im wunderschönen Monat Mai', set to music by Robert Schumann in his song-cycle *Dichterliebe*.

[23] See 7th July 1929 letter, p.89, regarding Ferenczi deserting the heat of a Budapest summer for the cool of the mountains in St. Moritz, Switzerland.

[24] 7th IPA Congress in Berlin from 25th to 27th September.

[25] Reference to the growth of the International Psychoanalytic Association.

[26] 'Organic failure' is a suggested translation to make sense of an otherwise recondite sentence in the German. 'Inkompensationen' may mean the inability of the body to compensate when parts go wrong, as happens in heart disease.

[27] In fact, at the Congress, Groddeck ended up presenting a paper titled 'Die Flucht in die Philosophie'. ('The Flight into Philosophy' in *International Journal of Psycho-Analysis*, 1923, 4, p.373f.)

[28] The Groddecks had been on holiday in the Black Forest since the beginning of January in Murberg, near Sasbachwalden, some 20 km. south of Baden-Baden. His mailing address was c/o H. Zink.

[29] Groddeck's sanatorium on the hill in Baden-Baden has now become a hotel − 'Hotel Tanneck'.

[30] A Swedish widow, Emmy von Voigt (1874-1961), née Larsson, became Groddeck's second wife and assistant. Groddeck met Emmy in 1915 when she became his patient, and they married in 1923. She was a trained masseuse.

Sándor Ferenczi to Georg Groddeck

Budapest, 2nd May 1922

Dear Groddeck,

We're worried that the letter containing my wife's enquiry about the possibility of her daughter[1] staying with you (throughout

August) may have got lost.[2] And then there's your long overdue reply to an interminable letter of mine. Permit me to suggest, therefore, that you give yourself a jolt in order to overcome your resistance to replying, particularly as we (my wife and I) are, so to speak, dependent on you, not least because we intended to spend part of the summer as paying guests or rather, as your patients.

Please put my mind at rest quickly, and with kindest regards to you and Frau von Voigt,

I remain your devoted friend

Ferenczi

[1] Elma Laurvik.
[2] Gizella did not add a postscript to the letter of 27th February 1922. There appears to have been another letter which is missing.

Sándor Ferenczi to Georg Groddeck

Budapest, 8th May 1922

Dear Groddeck,

All the arrangements are now made. My wife's daughter (her name is Elma Laurvik) will arrive in Baden-Baden at the beginning of August – from San Francisco, where she now lives. It is not certain, though, that she will be going back there, as her marriage is in quite a mess.[1] She is not well-off, but she has at her disposal sufficient funds to cover the cost of her treatment.

A simple room would suit her best. I'm quite sure she will feel at home with you and make a good recovery.[2]

You have said that one should be open about one's financial situation. I quite agree with you, and will therefore tell you right away that I have saved enough during the past working year to be able to continue – in keeping with a psychoanalytic rule – my treatment with you as a proper patient. I don't think my wife requires any specific treatment.

We intend staying from the end of August or early September until the beginning of the Berlin Congress.

I'm already greatly looking forward to seeing you again, and talking again[3] (but not against[4] you!).

Yours,

Ferenczi

P.S. Best wishes to Frau von Voigt! – from me too.[5] I want to thank you, dear doctor, for your letter. I can hardly wait for Elma to be with you, as I am convinced you will become very close.

Looking forward to a happy reunion,

Yours,

Gizella Ferenczi

---

[1] Elma had married an American, Hervé Laurvik, a writer of Swedish-American extraction. The marriage was not happy and they separated after only a few months in the summer of 1918, but never divorced. In her letter to Michael Balint of 7th May 1966, Elma wrote that of all the men in her life, 'it is my husband I loved the best, but he was a kind of Peer Gynt, who brought our life to a disaster' (Dupont, 1995).

[2] Frédéric [Frigyes] Kovács's letter of 8th January 1927 relates that Elma, according to Emmy, 'war nahe am Erlöschen' – 'was close to dying'. See Appendix 1, p.120.

[3 and 4] A play on two identically pronounced German words: 'wieder' (again), and 'wider' (against), that is, 'wieder sprechen' and 'widersprechen'. Cf. Engl. 'again' and 'agin'.

[5] Gizella takes over at this point.

Georg Groddeck to Sándor Ferenczi

Baden-Baden, 9th May 1922

Dear Ferenczi,

Before I go any further, I must tell you that letters went off to you and your wife some 10 days ago telling you of our joy at the prospect of seeing you again and expressing the hope that your stepdaughter's treatment would be a success. I hope that both letters, which crossed yours, have since arrived. They also included my thanks for sending the collected essays.

Now a few words about the resistance to putting pen to paper. In your last letter you wrote about your stay in Vienna and your sessions with Freud. Your letter arrived at the very moment when all sorts of difficulties with my book had accumulated, putting me in a bad mood. You had been telling me about your 'resistance to writing' when a friendly but firm-sounding letter from Rank arrived, which made me think about this Freud-complex and I hit on the solution. I'm now going to go back a few months. On reading my 'Letters to a Woman Friend', Freud wrote to me that it didn't seem quite right to him where I was heading, as this could easily lead to unbridled behaviour and disloyalty, and he held Stekel's name up to me as a warning. I know little about Stekel, having only read his *Sprache des Traumes*[1] and a few things in volumes of the *Zentralblatt*.

On the other hand I did know about Freud's reservations regarding Stekel's character, and knew from you that Stekel had the habit of claiming as his own intellectual property things he had got from Freud and others.

26

In the 'Letters to a Woman Friend' I did an endless amount of pilfering myself, but considered myself – and still do – perfectly entitled to do so. In pinching from Stekel, for example, I 'stole' his symbolism of numbers, and what is more in a pretty ridiculous way – and I'm not very happy about the rest of the book either. But particularly this symbolism of numbers, or at least the way I applied it, met with antagonism in Vienna, and because I felt hurt, I growled and barked at Freud and Rank, at the publishing company and Viennese psychoanalysis in general, and as for you, I simply refused to mention you. That's over now, I'm a good boy again and it only remains for me to thank you for helping me back onto the right path once again.

[At this point, a handwritten note by Groddeck's executor, Margaretha Honegger, states: 'The above is a handwritten draft of a letter to Ferenczi. Whether it was sent in this form cannot be established.']

[1] Munich, 1911; English title: *Interpretation of Dreams*, (Liveright, NY., 1943).

Sándor Ferenczi to Georg Groddeck

Budapest, 8th July 1922

Dear Groddeck,

You've only yourself to blame that I can recommend no better spa and holiday resort than Marienhöhe to my people.[1] My wife's daughter, whose intended arrival I've already announced in previous letters, will in fact be with you on August 1st.[2] We have just heard from my sister-in-law, Frau Otto Morando,[3] in

Hamburg that she would like to see us in Baden-Baden. Would you be so kind as to take her under your trusty wing; she is in dire need of your care. I will also be coming, together with my wife, towards the end of August or early September, and intend staying until the Congress.[4] I will be spending the month of August in Seefeld/Tyrol with the Ranks,[5] and will have to take along an English colleague, a lady who is not free at any other time.[6]

I can't wait to see and hear you talking again.

Please write, if only a card, by return of post (I mean it!), just to let me know you have got this letter.

My best wishes to Frau von Voigt; likewise from my wife, of course.

Yours,

Ferenczi

Bpest, VII Nagydiófa utca 3

---

[1] Ferenczi often referred patients and friends to Groddeck's sanatorium.

[2] Elma signed into the sanatorium guestbook as arriving 31st July and departing 17th September 1922. She then later returned, signing into the guestbook 30th September and staying until 15th December 1922.

[3] Frau Otto Morando (Sarolta), née Altschul, Gizella Ferenczi's sister, signed into the sanatorium guestbook 6th August and stayed until 17th September. Like Elma, she too returned to the sanatorium, staying from 18th October until 20th December 1922.

[4] The Ferenczis signed into the guestbook 25th August and stayed until 20th September 1922. See also p.23, n.24.

[5] Otto and Beate (Tola), Otto's first wife. The Ferenczis and the Ranks stayed at Seefeld. Abraham and Sachs visited them during their stay.

[6] Ferenczi, like other analysts at that time, would often see patients during his holidays.

Sándor Ferenczi to Georg Groddeck[1]

Budapest, 11th October 1922
$$11+10+19+22 = 62 : 2 = 31^2$$

Dear Friend,

I am not surprised that – as you put it – the analytic fruits obtained from the material unearthed by so much emotional agitation should be so meagre. I don't believe in self-analyses. The unconscious is clever enough to mislead one at precisely the most salient points. Analysis requires that one gives the self a certain amount of rein which is not possible when one permits a large part of one's psychoanalytic abilities to reign as the critical authority – which is the case in self-analysis, where one tries to be father and son at one and the same time. Partial analyses are perhaps possible in this way, but they will, at most, only serve to give a deeper or broader understanding of what one already knows. Intrinsic new insights about oneself cannot be reached in this way. That would require the 'simmering heat of transference', which just isn't there in self-analysis.

The analyses of numbers which appear to be so striking permit of two explanations: 1) the unconscious selects those important dates in a biography which somehow go arithmetically with a specific number; 2) once it has appropriated such a number, it can indeed shift important events onto corresponding dates of the calendar. Other, equally important, events are simply ignored if the number doesn't fit them.

Analysis is, in my opinion, a social phenomenon. It requires (at least) two people. It is, after all, merely a more successful

29

re-run of one's original upbringing, that is, dealing with the emotional relationship with one's parents.[3]

The main objection to this argument will surely be that <u>Freud</u> himself practises self-analysis. The response has to be: 1) that it is simply an argument about authority, or one 'ad hominem';[4] 2) that we know the content of <u>Freud's</u> self-analysis from his *Interpretation of Dreams*: we know how deeply he probed beneath the surface; and yet we cannot judge how complete his self-knowledge is or how evenly he plumbs the depths; 3) one can of course concede the possibility of self-analysis in the case of <u>extremely rare</u> individuals who are able, as it were, to take themselves to court and subject themselves to scrutiny. But that in no way affects the general validity of the rule which Freudian analysis demands.

That self-analysis actually offends against the rule of 'sociality' is also proven by the following facts: 1) Mentally ill people who, as a result of an alteration in their psychic structure, split themselves off from society (become asocial) are genuinely able to analyse themselves, that is, empty the contents of their unconscious effortlessly without the help of an obstetrician. 2) Even a person who has not been analysed or who has been inadequately analysed can analyse <u>someone else</u>;[5] and by way of this <u>projection</u> analyse himself (as can a paranoid person who is not wholly demented). 3) Similarly, many people project their personal complexes into scientific discoveries (as has been noted in my own case!). There are clearly countless ways in which self-analysis can come unstuck.

Consequently, someone (like yourself) undergoing such intensive self-analysis should at least follow it up with a proper analysis, to show him where he went wrong. Otherwise he will proceed in a perhaps partly vicious circle and fuse genuine insights with erroneous ones. There is no need for exceptional ability on the part of the analyst; he can be less clever than the analysand and yet discover things in him to which the latter was blind.

I am writing all this in order to urge you to accept my invitation to come to Budapest and continue here the analysis you have already embarked upon.[6] Whether and how far this will be compatible with the simultaneous analysis of myself, remains to be seen.[7]

I was pleased to hear your opinion about my Budapesters.[8] Hollós[9] is a very nice person. He wants to achieve 'great things,' but is very confused; left to his own devices he can't cope at all.

Best wishes from us to Frau Emmy – and for your birthday on the 13th.[10]

Your Ferenczi

Having got to the end of this letter I realise that instead of a letter I've written a scientific tract, and I have quite failed to take up many of your observations.

'The tangled braids' is not a bad metaphor.[11] However, I think there's no harm in temporarily curbing youth's excessive imagination and desire to discover something new at all costs. I'd let what is right in Freud's oeuvre consolidate itself a bit first. It would be terrible if after all the trials and tribulations involved in more or less categorising insights they should be upset and phantastically reshuffled by scientific Hattingbergs.[12] If there is no order in thinking one cannot attain even so much as an intimation of understanding. There are, of course, poets and

31

founders of religions, and prophets too, who have no need of systematised knowledge and still have the right ideas about many things (mixed up with as many errors). We don't object that there are such people; we even concede that there is <u>much</u> we can learn from them. But why, in God's name, should these people entangle their individual mode of working with ours into an inextricably knotted ball? We'll do without prophesy, and are happy to leave it (without envy) to those poets, though there are exceptions (see <u>Freud</u>) who are very able to harmonise the prophetic with the critical.[13]

Consequently (although a revolutionary by nature myself) I am all for retaining the braids you so denounce. The time will come when these braids will disentangle themselves, to centre around something else. Give scientific ideas a bit of space, time and protection! – that's what I desire.[14]

Now a bit about me. In Baden-Baden we were (in my opinion too exclusively) preoccupied with my kidneys, and very much neglected my strange breathing problems which continue to per-sist (always at night: Cheyne-Stokes[15] or very shallow breathing with repercussions the following day.)

My session hours are gradually filling up – though for the time being only with patients with Hungarian money;[16] the English woman who asked to see me hasn't turned up yet. We read with horror about the devaluation of your currency. Where will it all end?

Your F.

Dear Doctor – I'm only sorry that I cannot give you a third kiss on your birthday. Sending Emmy and you my best regards,

Your Gizella F.

[1] First letter to employ the familiar 2nd person singular form of address – thou/Du/tu.
[2] This sequence of numbers is obviously based on the date: 11/10/1922. However it is not clear about the significance of the 62 and the 31. Ferenczi does not allude to the number 31; but at the end of his letter he wishes Groddeck a happy birthday for the 13th of the month. Could Ferenczi's number play have anything to do with Groddeck's explorations of numbers as symbols and his 'Zahlenanalysen' [Analyses of numbers]?
[3] Ferenczi's approach was moving more towards this notion of therapy as a kind of re-parenting. Freud accused Ferenczi of trying to re-mother his patients: 'He wanted to show me how lovingly one has to treat one's patients in order to help them... so he himself became a better mother' (*Freud-Jones Correspondence*, 29th May 1933, p.721).
[4] 'ad hominem', that is, Freud is a case all of his own, and arguments which apply to him should not be taken as having general validity. For Ferenczi's critical views of Freud's self-analysis, see his 1932 *Clinical Diary*: Ferenczi writes of Freud's 'fear of allowing himself to be analysed' (p.185). See also Dupont's (1988) introduction to the *Diary* (p.xxiii). Interestingly, for a very different perspective of Ferenczi's view of Freud's self-analysis which flatters Freud as the great man who is able to do self-analysis, see his letter of 26th December 1912 to Freud (*Freud-Ferenczi Correspondence*, Vol. I, p.449). It is worth noting in this discussion of the sociability of psychoanalysis, Freud's own comment in a 21st December 1924 letter to Groddeck: 'It is difficult to practice analysis in isolation. It is an exquisitely sociable undertaking' (*The Meaning of Illness*, p.90).
[5] This can be interpreted as an allusion to the kind of mutual analysis Ferenczi was later to engage in with one of his patients – Elizabeth Severn – code-named 'R.N.' in his diary. In fact, his statement seems to support a general notion of mutual analysis.
[6] In a letter to Freud (31st May 1923) Groddeck says Ferenczi analysed him 'about six or seven times' in 1922 (*The Meaning of Illness*, pp.81-82).
[7] Specific allusion to the idea of some form of mutual analysis with Groddeck. In his 1932 *Clinical Diary*, Ferenczi writes at length about his experiment in mutual analysis with Elizabeth Severn.
[8] The Hungarian Psychoanalytic Association. Founded by Ferenczi in 1913, some of the more notable members included Géza Róheim, Michael Bálint, and Imre Hermann.
[9] István Hollós (Heszlein) (1872-1957), a psychiatrist, friend of Ferenczi and clinical director of the Budapest psychiatric hospital (asylum) Lipótmezö (known as the 'Yellow house'). He was a founding member of the Hungarian Psychoanalytic Association (1913). Probably one of the first psychiatrists to use psychoanalysis to understand psychosis (Haynal, 1988). He introduced psychoanalytic treatment methods into institutional psychiatry. In 1926, he published a novel about life in a psychiatric hosptial as seen through the eyes of a psychoanalyst: *Farewell to the Yellow House* (Hinter der gelben Mauer) – a classic of humanistically inspired reform in psychiatry (published in French in Le Coq Heron, Paris, no.100). With Ferenczi, in 1922, Hollós co-wrote the book *Psychoanalysis and the Psychic Disorders of General Paresis* (Zur Psychoanalyse der paralytischen Geistesstörung, Leipzig, 1922). He became president of the Hungarian Psychoanalytic Association after Ferenczi's death in 1933.
[10] Groddeck was 56 years old on 13th October 1922.
[11] 'The tangled braids' ('die verknoteten Zöpfe'). It seems likely that Ferenczi is referring to a mixed metaphor employed by Groddeck in a previous letter. The German

idiom 'die alten Zöpfe' alludes to old and outmoded, often uninspired and erroneous customs and ways of thinking. See also Groddeck's reply of 12th November 1922 below, where he speaks disparagingly of 'braided colleagues' (p.37).

[12] Dr. Hans Ritter von Hattingberg (1879-1944), German Doctor of Law and Medicine and psychoanalyst member of the Munich branch society. Hattingberg later became a member of the Aryanized German General Medical Society for Psychotherapy and of the German Institute for Psychological Research and Psychotherapy in Berlin. Hattingberg's name is mentioned disparagingly in letters between Groddeck and Freud, 1922-25 (*The Meaning of Illness*, pp.76-93).

[13] This section reflects Ferenczi's non-scientific interests, yet affirms his commitment to putting psychoanalysis on a 'scientific' footing.

[14] Ferenczi is committed to 'science' whereas Groddeck does not trust 'science' and actively intends to cultivate his not knowing of some things. This opposition around the 'scientific' is an ongoing point of contention between them.

[15] Ferenczi writes of this particular breathing pattern in his *Clinical Diary* (pp.6, 133-134). 'The Cheyne-Stokes respiratory pattern is an abnormal pattern of respiration that occurs in cases of severe uraemia. Periods of apnoea alternating with periods of deep, rapid breathing. The respiratory cycle, which begins with slow, shallow breaths, increases to abnormal depth and rapidity, then subsides, climaxing in a period of ten to twenty seconds without respiration, before the cycle is resumed.' – Ed. Judith Dupont.

[16] Ferenczi uses the phrase 'Kronen-Patienten' ['crown-patients'].

Georg Groddeck to Sándor Ferenczi

Baden-Baden, 12th November 1922

Dear Sándor,

Having waited till today before replying to your treatise of 11th October I have the advantage, as you will have forgotten by now what you wrote. I will ignore the question of self-analysis and its fruits, as I have little to say on this matter, because I find the term quite meaningless. As far as I'm concerned, life itself is the main analyst, and what we doctors contribute is no more than a pathetic presumption. We are instruments without a will, used by life for some forever inscrutable ends. Whenever kindly fate sends me this fleeting insight I feel happy and elated, irrespective

34

of what else is going on in or around me. Now I can't see why life shouldn't use me as an instrument in my own analysis just as it would in the analysis of someone else. If you bide your time, you get results.[1] My last illness, which initially produced such meagre material, suddenly overwhelmed me with a flood of memories, interpretations, and so-called insights. I am very pleased about this.

I think the difference between us is that you are compelled to want to understand things, whilst I am compelled not to want to understand.[2] In other words – borrowing from current psycho-analytic terminology – I am happy to remain in the dark, in the imago of the womb, which you wish to escape. With such opposing drives we'll never run out of conversation material, a guarantee for lasting friendship. We will always have something to argue about. You, for example, assume that successful analysis requires a paternal transference. But why should the transference onto the mother, or onto the playmates, or the milk bottle, or rhythm or a rubber doll and the rattle be less efficacious?[3] I happen to like the indefinable, prefer to have my doubts, and, above all, love being looked after.[4] That's why it suits me to invent the It. I have the feeling that you enjoy laughing, which I also love doing. So why should we take what is termed scientific so seriously? It seems to me that science stops at the very moment it becomes codified into a rule or a law. The process of making laws is, in my view, so far advanced in our field of expertise that essential matters can no longer be discovered by convinced analysts, but only by the doubters, among whom I count Freud, you, and myself. Freud is inhibited by his unfortunate belief in the absolute necessity of assigning names, of labelling, but makes up for it through his genius. You've got plenty of that as well, but are bent on recognition, and fail to notice that the pompous aura surrounding the grown-up's godforsaken head,[5] to ensure that nothing goes in or comes out, is in the eyes of us children no more than a game, thank God, only play.

In the final analysis, I actually produce nothing myself, I am much too maternal, too inclined towards receiving and letting things develop naturally. The games I played with my sister,[6] who by the way was older than me, were called Mother and Child, and I was almost always the mother. Alternatively one could say that I am a digesting machine which consumes other people's ideas, releasing them again as a sausage after due assimilation, so that it requires a lot of work and insight to recognise the various elements in their former guise.[7]

You don't like the analyses of numbers;[8] they may indeed be wrong; but who cares as long as they're useful. And you can't for the life of me convince me that you haven't experienced their efficacy.

And now to the sentence which annoys me: 'Analysis is a social phenomenon, a re-run of one's original upbringing.' Yes, that's unfortunately what it amounts to, but we do it not for positive reasons but because we are vain, and we often create untold damage with our re-educating efforts. Anyone who can refrain from trying to improve either himself or others is truly a Messiah.

That we project our own complexes into scientific discoveries is self-evident. How else could we possibly discover anything?

Now to the last bit of your letter: no one could be more excited about continuing my analysis than I am. You presumably don't even know what I am expecting from it. But that is something personal. The only reason why our braided[9] colleagues insist on the analysis of every aspirant is to emphasise: we clever people don't need it, none of them has been analysed. But you lot are stupid, so come here and see how wise men can ape what Freud says – without understanding him – about Oedipus, totem and taboo, theories of infant sexuality, anal and castration complexes. 'The world is round, and I am the centre,' is what Aunt Anna[10] likes to say, and this is presumably what all people think. Freud calls it narcissism. I hope he has not forgotten how to laugh.[11]

Will my visit to Budapest come off? I don't know. It lies in the lap of the gods. For the moment it very much looks as if I won't be getting a holiday at all. One of my acquaintances has decided to get a teratoma,[12] which is inoperable, and now claims that I can treat him. Presumably he has heard that it's easier to die at the Marienhöhe than elsewhere.

Give my regards to Gizella, and tell her that her daughter and her sister are pleasant people whom it is a pleasure to treat.[13] You will of course be able to convince yourselves soon that Elma is none the worse for her stay here. What, however, has happened to your memory? We spoke a lot about your breathing problems, only you didn't tell me the whole story. But that's life, repression is what it's about.

Emmy looks dazzling; I wish you could see her now.

With affectionate greetings from us both. In loyal friendship,

Groddeck

[1] Essentially these lines encapsulate Groddeck's 'It' philosophy. His belief in a guiding life force and in fate ('Schicksal') seems to be in contrast to Freud's conflict model of the psyche. Groddeck's faith was in the 'It/Id', whereas Freud emphasised the

strengthening of the Ego. Freud developed 'an increasingly firm stance in favour of the intellect, the expression of [his] hostility toward the "Id" ' (Sabourin, 1985, p.167).

[2] Here Groddeck defines what he sees as the differences between himself and Ferenczi, yet he acknowledges the attraction and the promise that these differences make for an enduring friendship.

[3] Groddeck's idea here marks an early suggestion of what we have come to know, as defined by Winnicott, as the 'transitional object'. (Thanks to Eva Brabant for drawing this to my attention.)

[4] A graphic description of Groddeck's desire and propensity to be cared for and 'mothered' in the most direct form, can be found in his own words in his letter of 23rd November 1922 to Freud (unpublished).

[5] Literally: 'the big hat of the grown-up, which surrounds his damned head' – 'der grosse Hut des Erwachsenen, der dessen verdammtes Haupt umgibt'.

[6] Lina Groddeck (1864-1904). Groddeck was very close to her.

[7] In a fascinating portrait of Groddeck, which includes an analysis and interpretation of these comments, Roustang (1982) sums up Groddeck's position: '[Groddeck] could not position himself within the logic of the paternal transference... [but] instead, he remained within the indeterminate area of the maternal transference' (p.128).

[8] See Ferenczi's letter of 11th October 1922.

[9] This word in German would have associations of 'bewigged', i.e. old-fashioned, dyed-in-the-wool academics. See n.11 to Ferenczi's letter of 11th October 1922, p.33, about the 'tangled braids'.

[10] 'Tante Anna' – the German female equivalent to 'Joe Bloggs' or 'Joe Blow', i.e. the average, typical person.

[11] François Roustang picks up the theme, a reference to Freud, in 'Has he forgotten how to laugh?', the title of his chapter on Groddeck in his book *Dire Mastery* (1982), which explores the theme of discipleship in psychoanalysis.

[12] teratoma = a tumour, made up of various types of tissue, including tissues not usually found in the organ in which the tumour arises, including the three embryonic germ layers. It may or may not be malignant. Ferenczi makes extensive use of this term, medically and metaphorically. See Stanton (1991) for a detailed description of Ferenczi's and Groddeck's use of the term 'teratoma'.

[13] See n.2 and n.3, p.28.

Sándor Ferenczi to Georg Groddeck

Budapest, 11th December 1922

Dear Georg,

You can see how our opinions diverge overall in our views on the usefulness of discussion as such. You enjoy arguing for the sake of it and hope that longevity will allow us to keep arguing. I, on the other hand, am of the opinion that discussion does nothing to clarify the problems in hand. On the whole the disputants persist stubbornly in their point of view, are unapproachable, and love listening only to their own voice. In analysis too we have the established principle of not being drawn into discussion. If one refrains from pointing out a contradiction, then what was said, insofar as it has any value and force at all, will continue to have its effect. I think we were wrong to stray into an area so alien to psychoanalysis – to try to convince each other by means of 'arguments'. Even maestro Freud occasionally used to say: 'Arguments are two a penny!'[1] Don't you think it would be better to stop firing at each other, listen to each other's views on various psychological questions, and wait till the accumulation of experience or a superior insight shows that one or other of us is right? I believe I have proved that I am not a stickler for principles and that I am always prepared to modify my views. You can rest assured then that no dogma will prevent me conceding that you're right – if a conviction matures in me again that you are.

I will, however, now make one exception to the rule of not entering into discussion. You write as follows: 'I think the difference between us is that you feel compelled to want to understand things, and I am compelled not to want to understand them.' There are quite a few ambiguities in that remark. If what you mean is that I feel compelled to understand before being entitled to, then I must strongly object. I think I am sufficiently aware of the limits to what we can know; I think, too, that I am very strict in evaluating the reasons which compel me to form a judgment;

39

and, as you know, I am always prepared to adjust my thinking. I don't, however, deny that I incline towards wanting to understand, whilst admitting that complete understanding lies in the remote future and is probably unattainable. Your interests also lie in this direction, with the difference that you always stress this unattainability, whereas it is enough for me to accept the latter once and for all, and not let it stop me collating and categorising the little things we can know – knowledge of which gives such pleasure. And experience shows that this is no useless enterprise.

If you were right in the characterisation of your scientific method or mode of perception, then logically you would have to content yourself with repeating this one sentence (about the impossibility of knowing the It), which, incidentally, many philosophers have indeed done.[2] You don't do that, however; rather, you are concerned, as we disreputable 'academics' indeed are, to understand people, bodies and souls, and to heal them by means of this understanding. So you too work with the same instrument as I employ, namely with logic. It is wrong of you, then, to deny your own method of working and pretend that you work with some mystical, unfathomable daemon, or, to put it more accurately, with an instrument that has nothing to do with logic. Even if you guess at something unconsciously, you cannot dispense with (an admittedly different kind of) logic, the logic of the unconscious. I admit that every scientist actually works with the imagination, i.e. with the logic of the unconscious, i.e. he is originally a poet or artist. But why shouldn't he try to weave what is imaginatively devised into a world-view, i.e. compare it with what has been established, in other words: sort, measure

40

and classify experiences as far as possible. For the poet, too, classifies – if only with the help of symbolic (i.e. inexact) units of measure.

The poetic, intuitive desire to understand is still a desire to understand. The only person who can speak of not wanting to understand is the one who considers himself an automatic tool[3] (we all do this, by the way), who at the same time won't allow himself to notice what goes on within and around him. No 'normal' person does this, though; it seems, then, that man, in addition to his other drives, has a drive which compels him to understand both himself and the world. In a sense animals have a bit of this – so it isn't a despicable 'human invention'.

Let's be fair then and not fall into the other extreme: namely of denying any usefulness to logic, which was hitherto so over-rated. For then we would have to give up not only science, not only all conscious direction, but also speech and writing in particular, those transmitters of the conscious contents of knowledge.[4]

The main news in your letter was the regrettable fact that your holiday was ruined by the arrival of the patient who is so very ill. Before you start work again you should have a break and take a little trip – I still haven't given up hope of seeing you here.

Elma and Sarolta[5] write lovely things about you. We envy you the pleasant and childlike atmosphere which you have been able to create around yourself.[6] Out here in the world it's far more prosaic.

Very best wishes for Christmas and the New Year

from your Sándor Ferenczi

Best wishes for the New Year from me too! Elma will be with us in a few days and will have lots of lovely things to tell us about you – we are full of joyful anticipation.

Your Gisella F.

I hope your next letter will contain more <u>personal</u> news about yourself, which would be much nicer than all these endless boring discussions. Please write in detail about family matters, about the sanatorium, about your financial difficulties, etc., etc. How are things going with the Swedish *Everyday Life*?[7]

Your Sándor

[1] In German literally: 'Arguments are as cheap as blackberries.'

[2] The source for this notion of 'das Es' (It/Id) is still under debate. The usual understanding is that Groddeck borrowed the concept and term from Nietzsche. However, see the various arguments for the genesis of this term in psychoanalysis, in Bos (1992). Ferenczi seems to be trying to score a point in his debate with Groddeck by pointing out that his concept of the 'It' is *not* original.

[3] Literally: 'automatic tool' – 'automatisches Werkzeug'.

[4] This is a strong statement of Ferenczi's position regarding Groddeck's view of 'science', knowledge, and the intellect. It is interesting to see Ferenczi, who is usually characterised as a romantic, rail against the romance of the instinctual. However, here we see the Ferenczi who would defend Freud's position, i.e. a suspicion of the instinctual. One can also see Ferenczi's tendency to balance positions – sensing that Groddeck is too far inclined towards the instinct. Generally, Ferenczi tends to challenge extremes (also in himself) and to suggest the dangers in overemphasising any position. He does this in his later critique of psychoanalysis as overemphasising fantasy at the expense of the traumatic reality in work with patients.

[5] See the reference to Elma's and Sarolta's stay at Groddeck's sanatorium on p.37 in Groddeck's letter of 12th November 1922.

[6] Life at Groddeck's sanatorium included regular celebrations, birthday parties, and dressing up in costumes for impromptu theatrical stagings. All the guests, i.e. patients, were involved.

[7] Emmy Groddeck was translating Freud's *Psychopathology of Everyday Life* into Swedish. Freud called her 'my charming translator' (see *The Meaning of Illness*, p.76 and p.106; but see also Freud's letter to Ferenczi of 13th September 1924). This last sentence was omitted in earlier editions.

Sándor Ferenczi to Georg Groddeck

Budapest, 19th February 1923

Dear Georg,

If I recall correctly it is today that you will be opening the gates to the Marienhöhe; at least I think that's what you wrote in your last letter to Elma. I will thus use the occasion to commiserate with you, although I know from my own case that after being on holiday for some time one can actually look forward to working again.

The desire to work is not very pronounced with me and is restricted to the eight or nine analytic hours required to earn my daily bread (and cake). These hours are, however, extremely interesting. – I spend the rest of the time being ill; that is, only really since one of my patients (Frau Dr. Radó-Révész,[1] whom you knew) died whilst undergoing analysis from progressive pernicious anaemia,[2] which she developed upon the death of her father, with whom she had a love-hate relationship. (Her husband,[3] who is undergoing analysis in Berlin, didn't and doesn't know about this analysis of his wife.) This patient, moreover, was six to seven months pregnant. When her blood count was down to 600,000 red corpuscles and she was oedematose,[4] the doctors performed a sectio caesarea, which she only survived by two days – the child by eight.[5]

It was just before her demise that I experienced new heart symptoms (irregular pulse) and an intensification of my old insomnia, as well as my nightly apneustic attacks[6] and drop in body temperature,[7] etc. – in a word, the death-wish. Despite this

43

state I still made a trip to Kaschau[8] (formerly Hungary, now Slovakia), where I gave two lectures. On my return I continued with being ill, experimented with head-baths, took up the well-proven stomach pressing,[9] and even went as far as to reach for quinine-strychnine pills.

I was, however, eventually able to pull myself sufficiently together to do a bit of self-observation, and established a clear parallelism between my respective attitude at a given moment within the triangle[10] $\begin{smallmatrix} & S & \\ E & \triangle & G \end{smallmatrix}$ and my state of health. This resulted in a certain improvement and had a calming effect – and, on the other hand, produced a new scientific theory which I won't withhold from you.

I believe that so-called bronchial asthma should simply be termed <u>Angsthma</u>[11] (of course this is only a joke). It is fear [Angst] which prevents exhalation and causes contraction in the respiratory passages. Compression of the pulmonary capillaries causes more or less severe blockages in the pulmonary circulatory system – and anaemia in the systemic circulatory system[12] – as well as heart problems.

But this isn't the new bit. What's new is my assumption that an <u>epileptic fit</u> probably isn't triggered by the brain, but should be considered as an exceptionally strong asthma attack, at least as far as the mechanism is concerned.[13] Common parlance would once again be right in describing epilepsy as heart-cramp. The cerebral functions are only affected secondarily. The sequence of symptoms would thus run as follows: 1. Breathing paroxsyms; 2. blockage of the lungs with oedema; 3. blackouts; 4. seizures.[14]

So much for the physiology. But what is the <u>meaning</u> of it all, what does its psychic content represent? This may and indeed

44

has to be strongly 'overdetermined'. At least <u>one</u> of the meanings of such an attack (as has long been suspected, of course) is its representation, its experiencing of coitus, and, furthermore, in the role of the penis. The whole body becomes a penis; it gets an erection (it becomes stiff) + (full of blood), is thrown hither and thither; after ejaculation (lung oedema) it goes limp.[15]

You could interpret nightly asthma attacks similarly. Probably likewise many diurnal or chronic asthmatic conditions.

It is the lung seizure that causes the blackout, which then brings the <u>unconscious</u> to dominance.

Kindest regards,

Sándor

Very best wishes to Frau Emmy

I almost forgot to draw the therapeutic consequences. To arrest an epileptic attack one could apply your <u>stomach-kneeling</u> technique, rather than holding the nose closed, as I have attempted to do.[16] Try it out, perhaps on your Russian. Or have you perhaps already done so?

---

[1] Erzsébet Radó, née Révész (1887-1923), Hungarian neurologist and wife of psychoanalyst Sándor Radó. She was first analysed by Freud in 1918, then by Ferenczi. See also n.3 below.

[2] A blood disease. This was the illness that would kill Ferenczi himself almost exactly ten years later in May 1933. Interesting that here Ferenczi attributes a psychosomatic cause to the disease. He also ascribed at least a partial psychosomatic cause to the onset of his own pernicious anaemia in his letter of 20th March 1933 to Groddeck only months before his death (see p.105). He wrote that the disease was brought on in part by his 'disappointment in Freud'. He alludes to Freud's rejection of him (see also p.106, n.5).

[3] Sándor Radó (1890-1972), Hungarian psychoanalyst, lawyer and physician, a former pupil of Ferenczi and first secretary of the Hungarian Psychoanalytic Association

(1913). In 1922, Radó went to Berlin and into analysis with Abraham. Radó had a falling out with Ferenczi at some point. Ferenczi wrote that he felt 'abandoned by colleagues (Radó, etc.), who are all too afraid of Freud to behave objectively or even sympathetically towards me, in the case of a dispute between Freud and me' (*Clinical Diary*, p.212). Radó became editor of the *Zeitschrift* after Rank resigned, and emigrated to New York in the 1930s to become a prominent member of the New York psycho-analytic community, organising an analytic institute at Columbia University. His paper 'Das Problem der Melancholie' (1927) became a classic. For more on Radó, see Roazen and Swerdloff (1995).

[4] Oedematose, i.e. oedematous – in the form of an oedema. Pernicious anaemia is a blood disease which today is curable through massive doses of vitamin B12. At the time the treatment consisted of subcutaneous injections of liver extract.

[5] The death of this child, whose gestation occurred at the same time as the mother's analysis with Ferenczi, deeply touched Ferenczi, who often alluded to his wish for children and fantasies of pregnancy.

[6] Apneustic attacks are episodes of nocturnal apnoea, which is periodic cessation of breathing.

[7] See Christmas 1921 letter for more detail on Ferenczi's symptoms.

[8] Kaschau (aka Kassa) is a small town in northern Hungary about 200 km. from Buda-pest. From 1919 onwards Kaschau was a part of Slovakia.

[9] stomach pressing, i.e. 'Bauchdrücken' – another of Groddeck's treatment exercises.

[10] Ferenczi's drawing of the triangle confirms that he is referring to his complicated emotional relationship with his wife and her daughter Elma. Without the drawing of the triangle – it was not included in the earlier French and German publications – a first assumption might have been that a triangle existed between Radó, his wife and Ferenczi, given that Radó did not know that his wife was in analysis with Ferenczi, and that Ferenczi and Radó were not on good terms. However, it is possible that the sense of the triangular in the Radó situation evoked the situation in his domestic life. Also, the death of Mrs Radó's child was quite possibly a stimulating factor, since Ferenczi's own desire for children was frustrated by his choice of marriage partners – the older mother over the younger daughter. See Christmas 1921 letter.

[11] 'Angsthma' – fusion of 'Angst' and 'asthma'.

[12] The obstructive failure of the pulmonary circulation reduces the volume of oxy-genated blood reaching the rest of the body as the systemic circulation.

[13] Ferenczi wrote of these ideas in a posthumously published article 'On epileptic fits: observations and reflections' (written about 1921), *Final Contributions to the Problems and Methods of Psycho-Analysis*, pp.197-204.

[14] Ferenczi's theory on the relationship between asthma and epilepsy is not supported by present day medicine. Today, epilepsy is characterised by a disturbance of cerebral activity which can be detected by methods such as encephalograms.

[15] This is Ferenczi at his imaginative best, taking an unusual notion and exploring it with great flair. See Ferenczi's *Thalassa*, for a whole book based on such creative leaps.

[16] Ferenczi's idea of using the 'stomach kneeling' for treating an asthma attack would probably facilitate the present day technique of diaphragmatic breathing, emphasising expiration of the breath.

Sándor Ferenczi to Georg Groddeck

Budapest, 4th May 1923

Dear Georg,

I am only writing on a professional matter now. Ever since her son was killed in the war, a 47-year-old lady, wife of a Prof. at the institute of technology has been suffering from progressive symptons of paralysis agitans (characteristics: shaking, stiff posture, stiff walk, frozen facial expression, etc).[1] Therapy so far unsuccessful. I want to ask you whether, in this case, you would like to try out your combined physiological-psychoanalytical procedure, and whether you by any chance have any experience with this kind of thing. Perhaps the lady would agree to go to Baden-Baden. Please let me know soon!

I am just reading your letters about the It.[2] It is even nicer reading it in book form than from the manuscript.

I will probably have to review it for the *Zeitschrift*, which means that I will have to get my point of view across!

[Ferenczi's signature missing]

---

[1] 'Paralysis agitans' was the term coined, in 1817, by James Parkinson, to describe what is now commonly referred to by the eponymous term 'Parkinson's Disease'. The 'frozen facial expression' characterises the 'Parkinsonian mask' when the muscles go into a spasm, expression is lost, and the face becomes like a mask. The shaking in Parkinson's usually starts with a fine tremor – often a 'pill rolling' action involving the thumb and first finger. The co-ordination of normal movement is also lost.
[2] *The Book of the It* (1923), subtitled as 'Letters to an unknown woman'.

Sándor Ferenczi to Georg Groddeck

Budapest, 9th June 1923

Dear Georg,

I have an unusual explanation for my long silence this time: I had too much to say; and, what is more, it's about something very, very sensitive. I'll get straight to the point. Professor Freud is ill. He happened to notice a roughness in his palate. It was diagnosed as a 'leukoplakia',[1] that is, a flat tumour which had spread over the whole of the back left half of the palate, spilling over into the cleft of the upper jaw. The doctors and specialists (from whom neither the Professor nor Rank[2] could elicit an entirely clear diagnosis)[3] immediately said that it was essential to operate. They (that is, Prof. Hajek, a famous Viennese stomato-laryngologist)[4] removed the growth,[5] except for the bit in the jaw which is getting radium treatment. I was in Vienna over Whitsun, and found the Prof. mentally very alert, though extremely anaemic.[6] He wasn't pessimistic about his condition, but assumes that the doctors are withholding a diagnosis of epithelioma[7] from him. Nevertheless he is hoping for a positive outcome. – My own assessment of the case varies according to mood. Today, for example, things look extremely bleak. – I beg you not to mention any of this to anyone (Frau Emmy excepted).

My own (probably sub-sternal)[8] struma has become enlarged too and troubles me at night, leaving me with just enough energy for my nine daily working hours (necessary for earning my living). I have no time left for books.[9] – But I intend to stop work soon, so that I can really implement some of my long-cherished plans (getting on with the genital theory).[10] However, as I have to stay in direct contact with Rank because of the project[11] we are working on together, I will have to give up the idea of visiting you, agreeable though that would be, at least for this year, not least because I want to meet up with the Prof. (probably in southern Tyrol)[12] after seeing Rank.

I was right in thinking I would be chosen to review your *Book of the It*.[13] I will reserve this job for the holidays too. But this much I can already tell you, I will probably stress what I consider to be the particular merit of your approach: namely that you have never ceased emphasizing, along with the role of the father, the exorbitant importance of the <u>mother</u>.[14] Latest studies all point in this direction; of course, it was no bad thing from a scientific point of view (which you despise) that the idea of the importance of the parents developed historically in reverse order – in psychoanalysis too. Very little else to report from us. My wife is as always diligent and optimistic. Elma is somewhat bored, and consoles herself with occasional stomach pains. Sarolta, in Rome, has recovered from the eye trouble which plagued her for quite some time.

Foreigners are even more of a rarity here than in Baden-Baden. I have been invited to go to Oxford for the International Congress of Psychologists, but they forgot to include the necessary pounds.

Fondest greetings from both of us to you and Frau Emmy,

Your Sándor

---

[1] 'Leukoplakia' was a diagnosis made by Felix Deutsch (1884-1964), a Viennese internist, and by Maxim Steiner, an early member of the Vienna Psychoanalytic Society. See also p.50, n.3, and p.72, n.10.

[2] As well as being in Vienna, Otto Rank was very close to the Freud family – at this time probably even closer than Ferenczi (E. Falzeder, personal communication, Salzburg, February 1995).

[3] Deutsch had immediately recognized that Freud had a more advanced cancer, but, for whatever reasons, he withheld this information from Freud and pronounced the growth as a pre-cancerous leukoplakia.

[4] The surgeon was Prof. M. Hajek (1861-1941), Professor of Laryngology in Vienna. Hajek seemingly performed an excision of the leukoplakia, probably as an exploratory measure. His treatment of Freud was 'woefully inadequate' and approached negligence (Romm, S: *The Unwelcome Intruder: Freud's Struggle with Cancer*, New York, Praeger, 1983); see also Schur, M. (1972), *Freud: Living and Dying* (New York, International Universities Press), for more on Freud's cancer. Ferenczi, according to Jones (1957), was the only one to whom Freud confided his health problems.

[5] A hyperkeratinisation of the oral mucosa, with circumscribed yellowish-white leathery areas, possibly pre-cancerous.

[6] Freud had lost a lot of blood due to a number of haemorrhages associated with the surgery.

[7] Epithelioma – a malignant tumour in the skin epithelium.

[8] A form of goitre an enlargement of the thyroid gland presumably due to insufficient thyroid hormone production. It is normally found in the region of the throat, but here Ferenczi suggests it may be behind his sternum.

[9] Ferenczi frequently remarks about having little time left to write.

[10] *Thalassa: A Theory of Genitality.*

[11] A short book, *Entwicklungsziele der Psychoanalyse [The Development of Psychoanalysis]* (Nervous and Mental Disease Monograph Series No.40, 1925; German reprint of 1924 edition, Vienna: Turia & Kant, 1996), was co-authored with Otto Rank and at least in part written in Klobenstein. Consisting of six chapters, it discusses the interrelationship of psychoanalytic technique and theory.

[12] This meeting between Ferenczi and Freud did not come about. Ferenczi (with Gizella) and Rank were in Klobenstein writing their book and they had hoped to visit Freud for a few days in Lavarone before the Committee meeting (the first meeting to be held without Freud). However, they decided against a visit because they thought it might make the other Committee members jealous (E. Falzeder, personal communication, March, 1995, and Grosskurth, 1991, *The Secret Ring*, p.131).

[13] Again, Ferenczi doesn't seem to have reviewed the book for any psychoanalytic journal. Balint reviewed the book much later in 1951 for the *International Journal of Psycho-Analysis*, 32, pp.250-251.

[14] 'die exorbitante Bedeutung der Mutter' – Ferenczi's acknowledgement of Groddeck's recognition of the mother parallels Ferenczi's own influential views along these lines. In fact, Ferenczi, and the Hungarian school generally, are now recognised as a primary source for today's object relations theories. Since the development of the object relations perspective emerged out of the emphasis on the central relationship with the mother, Ferenczi may here be attributing to Groddeck a significant role in the development of his own thought, which to some extent opposes Freud's father-orientated views. Karen Horney also acknowledged Groddeck's influence in her critical work on the mother, gender and sex differences (Quinn, 1988, pp.216-218).

Sándor Ferenczi to Georg Groddeck

Klobenstein by Bozen[1] (now Italy), 5th August 1923

Dear Georg,

The Professor's news was not disheartening – although we still can't stop worrying about him.[2] I will be meeting him in the course of the summer not far from where he is currently staying (Lavarone, Trentino),[3] when I hope to hear more.

Baden-Baden seems less and less likely to be the venue for the Congress, given the current political situation.[4] Salzburg is on the cards, but nothing has been decided as yet.[5]

I am using my stay in beautiful but very hot Klobenstein to get my Genital Theory onto paper. It will make a book of about 100 pages.[6]

It will please you very much, I think, as will Rank's new book.[7]

A technical-scientific political book (which I'm doing with Rank) will be worked up along your lines of thought.[8] I am giving a daily session to an American lady I have brought along; otherwise I couldn't be spending all these *lire*.

I was consulted today by an interesting elderly Englishman. I sent him to you. I hope he will come.[9]

My wife is well. She helps me a lot with my writing.

My health has been improving for some time now. Occasionally I get (and feel) an 'extrasystole' of the heart.[10] My sleep is better, but not that good.

We will be going somewhere in the mountains next (Dolomites).

51

We often speak of Baden-Baden, about Frau Emmy, about you and everyone who grew dear to us there, and send you our fondest greetings.

Is Zsuka[11] still with you, or can't she bear being analysed? Our love to her too.

Your Sándor

Letters will be forwarded from here.

---

[1] Klobenstein (by Bozen) – now called Collalbo (by Bolzano) – is a small village in the Dolomite mountains of Trentino-Südtirol, northern Italy, about 11 km. from Bolzano. The region had been a part of the Austro-Hungarian Empire, but at the end of the First World War came under Italian rule. The names were changed during Mussolini's efforts to Italianise the region.

[2] Still referring to Freud's ongoing battle with cancer.

[3] Lavarone is a small town in the Trentino, Italy, which was a favourite place of Freud's. In late August, the Committee met at Castel Toblino between Laké Garda and Trento, travelling together to San Cristoforo, at the foot of the mountain where Freud was staying in Lavarone. After their stormy meeting – the first without Freud present – they went on to pay a last visit to Freud in Lavarone (Grosskurth, 1991, pp.131-133).

[4] The economic situation in Germany became evermore desperate in the wake of the Treaty of Versailles (1919). There was spiralling inflation, poverty and unemployment. National socialism gradually began to spread – the Nazi party had held its first party conference – and there was street-fighting amongst the various political factions. A number of eminent politicians had been murdered.

[5] The 1924 Eighth International Psycho-Analytical Congress did finally take place 21st-23rd April 1924 in Salzburg, the site of the first Congress sixteen years earlier. Since Freud was not able to attend due to his health, Groddeck lost interest in going to the Congress. Together with Robert Berény, Olga Székely-Kovács, younger daughter of Vilma Kovács, drew a series of 88 caricatures of the participants.

[6] See n.20, p.17, re: *Thalassa*. Freud also spent time writing in Klobenstein, where he apparently wrote *Totem and Taboo* (1913) ten years earlier in 1912-1913.

[7] *The Trauma of Birth*, New York: Harcourt, Brace, 1929. In German: Internationaler Psychoanalytischer Verlag, Leipzig/Vienna, 1924.

[8] *The Development of Psychoanalysis* (1925). See n.11, p.50.

[9] Reverend Arthur Meyrick, a 72-year-old English parson. See also next letter, 20th August 1923. Ferenczi had a number of English patients, as did Groddeck.

[10] An extra heartbeat. A heartbeat consists of the 'systole' when the ventricle contracts and the 'diastole' when it relaxes.

[11] Ferenczi's youngest sibling, Zsofia Erdös, née Ferenczi.

Sándor Ferenczi to Georg Groddeck

Klobenstein, 20th August 1923

Dear Georg,

Please find enclosed the address of Reverend Arthur Meyrick, a 72-year-old English vicar who suffers from cerebral circulation problems – imitating his father! His wife recently broke her arm, which has mended well, and then she got a swollen knee out of the blue. I advised them to see you immediately, and they would be grateful if you could let them know via me what would be the cost of full board and treatment.

The joint work is now finished.[1] I am convinced it will find approval. At the end of the month we're going to visit the Professor in Lavarone, and then I'll come back here, pick up my wife (who sends you both her greetings) and return home. I hope to be in Budapest around the 5th to 7th September.

Greetings from both of us also to Zsuka,

Your Sándor

[1] The book with Rank (see n.11, p.50).

Sándor Ferenczi to Georg Groddeck

16th September 1923, Bpest

Dear Georg,

Many thanks for your congratulations. This *Festschrift* business was rather premature. The impatient Hungarians were determined – whatever the price – to turn me into a Nobel prizewinner and seduced Freud and Rank into participating in this extravaganza.[1] At least it was a good opportunity for recollection and realising how unworthy I was of it. I hear that Zsuka, instead of getting well has decided she wants to become a psychoanalyst. Of course I won't support this wholly nonsensical plan.

Mrs. F. Révész[2] came home in a great state of excitement. How are things with the English vicar?[3]

I am terribly busy (9-10 hours daily), in order to make ends meet.

Best wishes from Gizella and myself to Frau Emmy and yourself.

Your Sándor Ferenczi

[1] A reference to Ferenczi's 50th birthday on 7th July. The event was commemorated by a Festschrift in the *Internationale Zeitschrift für Psychoanalyse*, Vol. 9.
[2] Flora Révész, wife of Budapest physician and psychoanalyst, Dr. Laszlo Révész, Secretary of the Hungarian Psychoanalytic Society. Mrs. Révész had been at Groddeck's sanatorium (6th Aug.- 9th Sept). The couple, together with their daughter, were shot by Hungarian Fascists in the 1940s.
[3] See n.9, p.52.

Sándor Ferenczi to Georg Groddeck

Budapest, 8th October 1923

Dear Georg,

I've only just realised that the birthday you are about to celebrate gives me the opportunity to return your congratulations on my 50th. You don't need my wishes for a ripe old age, because you could live forever, if you feel so inclined; and the same goes for good health, happiness and all those things the rest of us mortals so often hanker after in vain. It only remains for me then to tell you how happy I am that your It has seen fit to preserve you in such marvellous health and spirits. We are also happy to know you to be in the company of another It, so congenial to us, which doubtless can also lay claim to the honour of keeping you physically and mentally the person you are.[1]

I have, sadly, no good news to report about the Prof. A further radical operation is necessary after all – and what is more, any day now. The likelihood of the operation being successful is high. I saw the Prof. in Vienna a few days ago, and found him composed and in good spirits.

Proof-reading of the Gen. Theory and the joint work with Rank has begun.

> With best wishes to you,
>
> Your Sándor

The Prof. spoke of you with great warmth. Nevertheless, it might be better if you were to wait until after the operation before writing to him.

Dear Doctor, I too would like to wish you all the very best on your birthday. We will think of you with affection on the 13th.

> Best wishes from your ever grateful
>
> Gizella F.

Last and least it's me, Elma, writing to you. I too have such fond memories of your birthday that I can imagine you must be feeling wonderful. I wish you many, many such days. We would have loved to send you Hungarian salami and cheese, but nowadays it's almost impossible to do things by post. Hope we can make amends soon. I think of you and Emmy so often and embrace both of you,

Elma

[1] An allusion to Groddeck's wife, Emmy.

Sándor Ferenczi to Georg Groddeck

Budapest, 25th October 1923

Dear Georg,

I have the following to report on the Prof.'s condition: he underwent a preliminary operation (to ligate the right *carotis externa*).[1] Three or four days later they removed one third of his right upper jaw and a lamella of the lower mandible. A prosthesis was immediately inserted and the cavity covered with a skin transplant. The second operation lasted three hours.[2] The Prof. bore, and bears, it all heroically. After running a temperature for some days he recovered, and is to leave the sanatorium[3] for home at the end of the week. He is apparently well. The resected piece shows that everything diseased has been removed.[4] We are all hoping for the best.

I am up to my neck in work. To maintain a decent standard of living I have to work ten hours a day. But I am making good progress and am as absorbed by it all as I was seventeen years ago when I first began analysing.

We often think of you, especially now that your homeland, with which we sympathise so deeply, has hit on such hard times. Francophobia is widespread here, although the big powers seem to favour appeasement with this robber nation.[5]

Let's hear something jolly from you again.

To Frau Emmy and yourself our kindest regards,

Your

Sándor

---

[1] An artery which normally carries blood to nourish the head and face but is not indispensable if tied off.

[2] On 4th October, Freud had a pre-operation and on 11th October the radical surgery was carried out. Freud was fitted for a wooden jaw prothesis.

[3] Both operations were performed by Hans Pichler (1877-1949) at the Sanatorium Auersperg in Vienna. Pichler, a successful physician specialising in oral surgery, was to attend to Freud and his cancer for the next sixteen years until Freud's death.

[4] This, in fact, turned out not to be true. On 12th November, Pichler had to remove some further cancer. These operations were the first in a long series over the years.

[5] Hungarians 'hated' the French because at the end of the First World War they were the hardliners of the Treaty of Versailles, which – by taking great pieces of Hungarian land (approximately two-thirds) and changing boundaries – crushed Hungary.

Sándor Ferenczi to Georg Groddeck

Bpest, 30th June 1924

Dear Georg,

One thing is certain, it's my turn to write. The reason why I haven't written all this time is because I wasn't sure what I would be doing in the summer. An invitation to America was in the offing but fizzled out into being 'put on hold'.[1] We've now decided to spend the whole of July in a pension near Budapest[2] (as I will be working half days). We will probably go on from there to Switzerland, and eventually return home via Baden-Baden, where we want to spend at least two weeks.[3]

Things were pretty unpleasant at the congress in Salzburg, to say the least, though relative peace prevailed in the end.[4]

I was in Vienna last Sunday. Prof. Freud is able to work again. He shows no sign of a relapse, but is undernourished and weak. He's off to the Semmering any day now.[5]

I would be grateful if your friend Roeder[6] could get round to pointing out the most glaring mistakes in my 'Gen. Theory'.

I am pleased about your 'elasticity'[7] which I hope to experience myself this summer.[8] All things considered I'm feeling all right. During these holidays I want to write up 1) new aspects and possibilities of practical technical aids,[9] and 2) the connection between practical analysis and the genital theory.

Gizella, Elma, Sarolta, Zsuka, are well and send you both their best wishes. We often speak about Frau Emmy, and are, like you all, devoted to her.

Greetings from your Sándor

[1] A plan to join Otto Rank to work in America had just collapsed. Rank was at first enthusiastic about the opportunities for Ferenczi, but then cabled him that the situation was 'uncertain'. Ferenczi was disappointed since he had been making preparations to go to America (*Freud-Ferenczi Correspondence*, 30th June 1924). He eventually did go to the United States in the autumn of 1926.

[2] The Sanatorium 'Siesta' in Budapest I at Rath Georg-Str. 5.

[3] Although Sándor and Gizella did not sign the sanatorium guestbook for 1924, Ferenczi did write to Freud from Baden-Baden on 21st September.

[4] Ferenczi did not present a paper at the conference; however, there was a seminar on psychoanalytic theory and technique in response to Ferenczi's (and Rank's) ideas.

[5] Freud stayed at the 'Villa Schüler' on the Semmering – a hill with many surrounding hotels, approximately 100 km. southwest of Vienna.

[6] Egenolf Roeder von Diersburg (1890-1968), philosopher and philologist, appears in the sanatorium guestbook for 1923. Roeder wrote on Groddeck, and selected and edited Groddeck's writings in *Psychoanalytic Papers on Literature and Art*. He features briefly in the Freud-Groddeck correspondence (see *The Meaning of Illness*).

[7] Allusion to Ferenczi's idea which he develops in his 1928 paper, 'The elasticity of psycho-analytic technique' (S. Ferenczi: *Final Contributions to the Problems and Methods of Psychoanalysis*, pp.87-101).

[8] That is, in Baden-Baden (see also n.3).

[9] Throughout the second half of the 1920s Ferenczi devotes much of his clinical and theoretical work to an exploration of experiments in technique.

Sándor Ferenczi to Georg Groddeck

Budapest 11th October 1924

Dear Georg,

I'm working again – it's as if I'd never been in your little wooden house.[1] It's really horrid that work and pleasure have to be so sharply divided. How much nicer it would be if we could lighten our workload and make it more acceptable by the exchange of friendly words and sentiments. The R. affair continues – he no longer answers my letters, at least he hasn't so far.[2]

I'd love to be with you today right in the middle of all your well-wishers.

But next year – in Iceland[3] – we'll be together again, and what is more, to our heart's content.

Kind regards to dear Emmy and all our friends in Baden from your Sándor

Dear Doctor,[4] Many happy returns of the day – I often think with deep affection of Marienhöhe and of last year's 13th October – an exceptionally wonderful day – which seems as real now as then and as if I were in the middle of a beautiful fairy tale. I'd love to come back to the doctor for months on end in order to learn what I can from him for the years ahead. Unfortunately <u>for the time being</u> I cannot begin to afford it. Perhaps in a year or two. My best wishes to Frau Groddeck, to dear Eva and my friend Miss Spalding. I often think of the people I liked there, most of all of course the doctor, whom I embrace – if I may – with great love, respect and gratitude.

Zsuka

---

[1] This probably refers to Groddeck's small wooden house in the woods near Baden-Baden where he used to write. It was here that he wrote *The Book of the It*, and the spot is now called the 'Es-Punkt' by the Groddeck Society.

[2] In all likelihood 'R' refers to Otto Rank and his break with Freud and the 'Secret Committee'. See also above note 1, p.59, regarding Ferenczi's dashed hopes to join Rank in America. Rank had recently cabled Ferenczi this news.

[3] See following letter of 18th April 1925, on p.62, and note 4, p.63, regarding Iceland.

[4] Postscript from Zsuka, Ferenczi's youngest sister.

[Ed. comment: Probably an undated card from Ferenczi to the Groddecks should be placed here, at the very end of 1924.

On one side of the card there is a drawing of four figures – marked by Ferenczi as being Zsuka, Elma, Gizella and himself – walking up to a little house with presents. Ferenczi's message on the reverse of the card reads:

'<u>This</u> is how we would have liked to greet you on New Year's Day on the steps of your little house in the woods. Why won't you get in touch? What is happening about Iceland?']

Sándor Ferenczi to Georg Groddeck

Budapest 1925[1]

Dear Georg,
Herr von Bakonyi will be along today with Councillor Dr. Boros (a hospital director). The latter is a clever but totally non-analytically orientated physician, something which you will have to take into consideration when talking with him.

Do write!

Your

Sándor F.

[1]Date on card is illegible.

Sándor Ferenczi to Georg Groddeck

Budapest, 18th April 1925

Dear Georg,
The greetings you asked me to convey are warmly returned by all. As to our news, there's not much to relate.

My practice grows insofar as the number of Americans consulting me continues to rise, if slowly. I far prefer cases of neurosis, though, to the self-analyses of the so-called healthy or of my pupils. Anyhow, I have ample opportunity for gleaning new insights, which constitute the main pleasure of my otherwise uneventful and demanding life. My latest surprise is that I have

61

established the tremendous importance of the <u>foreskin</u>, which has hitherto been neglected. I want to present these things to the Homburg Congress,[1] so I won't explain them to you here. Indeed, I ask you to not raise the issue for the time being with anyone. Why? I will tell you that personally when the time comes.

Things have taken a turn for the worse in the Rank affair. A defeated hero upon his return from America, he then found his teaching posts in Vienna given to others. The fact that we recently wrote a book together created a lot of gossip about my relationship with the Prof. (with whom I remain, as ever, on the best possible terms). Rank is deeply depressed. Berlin[2] is *en vogue*.

One of my American ladies has a gentleman friend who I think belongs in the Marienhöhe. She has already written to him about it.

How is Herr von Bakonyi?[3] He hasn't written to me, even though he promised to do so. Would you still be able to fit in a (highly talented) Hungarian journalist with a kidney problem? And if so, what would be the minimum daily cost?

The Iceland idea seems to have evaporated, as you couldn't commit yourselves in any way.[4] That sort of thing needs to be planned well in advance, of course.

Our two holiday months are August and September, with the Congress[5] in between. I'll be working at half-steam the first month; and not at all during the second.

Kindest regards to dear Emmy and to you

from your

Sándor

[1] The 9th IPA Congress was held in Bad Homburg, near Frankfurt/Main, Germany, 3rd-5th September 1925. Ferenczi (1926) presented his paper 'Contra-indications to the "active" psycho-analytical technique' (*Further Contributions to the Theory and Technique of Psycho-Analysis*, pp.217-230). Specifically for Ferenczi's thoughts on the foreskin, see pp.227-228.

[2] Allusion to Karl Abraham and the Berlin psychoanalytic group. Ferenczi is being sarcastic in that he had a great antipathy towards this group. There was, at least from Ferenczi's perspective, a rivalry between the Budapest group and the Berlin group. This rivalry was based on differences of direction in psychoanalytic theory, practice and training.

[3] Karl von Bakonyi of Budapest was a patient at Groddeck's sanatorium from 8th March-27th July 1925, as noted in the sanatorium guestbook. He was probably a patient of Ferenczi who referred him to Groddeck for treatment.

[4] Thoughts about a trip to Iceland. Groddeck had also planned a trip to Sweden, where his wife Emmy was born.

[5] Bad Homburg (see n.1 above).

Sándor Ferenczi to Georg Groddeck

Budapest[1]

Winter and spring passed with a lot of practical work (rather more positive, from a therapeutic point of view, since the new technical aids). Apart from that, rather a lot of hypochondria and varying teeny-weeny symptoms.

My wife, Elma and I send you both our love,

Your

Sándor F.

[1] No date on this card; postmark illegible.

Sándor Ferenczi to Georg Groddeck

26th July 1925

Dear Georg and Frau Emmy,

Just to let you know that we shall be paying a short visit to the Professor at the Semmering on August 5th, and then arrive in Baden-Baden in the afternoon or evening.[1]

To a jolly reunion!

Your Sándor Ferenczi

---

[1] The Ferenczis signed into the sanatorium guestbook on the 5th August and stayed until 31st August.

Sándor Ferenczi *et al.* to Georg and Emmy Groddeck

Frankfurt, 5th September 1925

Dear Friends,

Sending our best wishes. The Congress went off all right.

Sándor

Gizella

Hope to see you soon!

Landauer[1]

Regards,

Meng[2]

(A further signature is illegible)

[1] Karl Landauer (1887-1945). Psychiatrist and psychoanalyst from Munich, who trained with Julius Wagner von Jauregg and was in analysis with Freud. Moving to Frankfurt in 1919, he founded the Frankfurt Psychoanalytic Institute with Meng in 1928. In 1933 he emigrated to Amsterdam. He was later deported to Belsen. For his writings, see Hans-Joachim Rothe, ed., *Karl Landauer: Theorie der Affekte und andere Schriften zur Ich-Organisation* [Karl Landauer: Theory of Affects and Other Writings on Ego Organization], (Frankfurt/Main, 1991).

[2] Heinrich Meng (1887-1972) was friendly with Ferenczi and frequently met up with Groddeck, both on a personal level and in the South-West German Psychoanalytical Study Group. Freud thought that, along with Franz Alexander, Meng was one of the brightest of the young analysts (Jones, 1957). He was an analysand of Paul Federn and Hanns Sachs, and was director of the Frankfurt Psychoanalytic Institute from 1928-1933, when he emigrated to Switzerland. Works include: *Psychohygienic Lectures*, Basel, 1960; *Psyche and Hormone* (ed.), Bern, 1960.

Sándor and Gizella Ferenczi to Georg and Emmy Groddeck[1]

10th September 1925

Dear Friends,

I'm writing to give you a foretaste of Italy. The day before yesterday, we went on an excursion to Nervi, and swam in the sea. I got 7 sea urchin thorns (?)[2] in my hand and foot. A beautiful Italian lady helped me pull them out – isn't that wonderful? Yes, it is! Weather fine. We embark at 10 am. today (and no symbolism intended!) Greetings and kisses as you will,

Sándor

Address, see above!

I embrace you both,

Your Gizella

[1] Postcard with handwritten address at top of card: Dr. S. Ferenczi, Hotel Quisisana, Capri (Italy) via Naples; on the reverse there is a picture of the ship 'Conte Rosso'.
[2] The term Ferenczi was looking for is 'spines'.

Gizella and Sándor Ferenczi to Georg and Emmy Groddeck

Sorrento,[1]
Hotel Vittoria
13th September 1925

Dear Friends,

What a surprise we got when we opened *The Ark*[2] today and saw my name in it! And how proud I felt that my birthday[3] gave you, dear – what shall I call you? You don't like 'Georg' and I don't like 'Pat'[4] – dear friend, the opportunity to incorporate so much of value to your readers. Makes one want to have a birthday every day when this is what happens.

After much prevarication we have ended up in Sorrento and haven't as yet regretted our decision, despite the bad weather. Every day we think of you with love and gratitude and look forward to our reunion – if but for a day[5] – on October 2nd – and then we're going to meet in Budapest! That's wonderful – wonderful – wonderful!!!

I embrace you both,
Gizella

I haven't been mentioned in *The Ark*, but I'm nevertheless delighted to be writing to you. Actually, I've almost forgotten about writing, that's how far removed I feel from everything connected with study. I'm leading a totally self-orientated exist-ence[6] – have several baths a day – sometimes salt baths, some-times ordinary; I eat and drink, albeit in small measure, which

66

isn't easy in view of the splendours on offer. At the moment I'm sleeping well on the whole and without problems. All's well with other bodily functions, too.

I now realise that having read something of Freud's yesterday what I have just written is nothing short of a lie; and I think I have hit upon a convincing supplement to his exposition on the function of judgment.[7]

With best wishes, and looking forward to seeing you soon,

Your Sándor

I heard many people praising your Homburg lecture[8] in very generous terms after you left.

---

[1] Sorrento, Italy. Small town south of Naples towards the tip of a peninsula on the Bay of Napoli.

[2] Groddeck had published a notice of Gizella Ferenczi's birthday in *The Ark* (*Die Arche*), a bi-monthly journal published by him predominantly for those at his sanatorium. Groddeck communicated his particular view as an 'organic' analyst through articles such as 'Resistance', 'Breathing', 'Psychoanalysis and the It', 'The thick neck'. There were three volumes of the journal from 1925 to 1927.

[3] Birthdays were a big occasion for celebrations at Groddeck's sanatorium.

[4] This was Groddeck's longtime nickname from childhood (see n.7, p.5).

[5] The Ferenczis had planned to meet the Groddecks in Venice, where they spent two days, on their way back from Naples and Rome. (E. Falzeder, personal communication, February 1995).

[6] In German – 'animalisches Dasein'; literally, 'animal existence'.

[7] Freud's paper titled, 'Negation' (S.E., 19).

[8] 'Psychoanalysis and the It', *Die Arche*, 1:10 (20.9.1925). Reprinted in *Psychoanalytische Schriften zur Psychosomatik* (Psychoanalytic Papers on Psychosomatics) ed. G. Clauser, Wiesbaden: Limes Velag, 1964.

[**Ed. comment**: Ferenczi gave a lecture to the Hungarian Psychoanalytic Society, 'How to know when active psychoanalytic technique should or should not be used', 24th October 1925]

Sándor Ferenczi to Georg Groddeck

Bpest, 6th December 1925

Dear Friend,

The day before yesterday a letter arrived from Freud in which he wrote of the great discomfort his otherwise small operation was giving him. That was <u>why</u> he couldn't talk to you for more than an hour.[1] He was feeling drained and disturbed in his activity all round. He mentioned his warm feelings for you, his appreciation of your discovery of the psychoan. influence on the organic, and of the importance you place on the 'It' in the org. process; but he was less happy with the way your ideas are <u>worked out</u>.

No particular news this end. We will probably go to Vienna over Christmas to discuss the contents of the journal's special edition with Radó[2] and some of the others.

As to my state of mind and body – *fluctuat nec mergitur*[3] – But on the whole somewhat improved.

Kovács[4] seems to be worse than ever. He's in agonies if he walks for more than ten minutes. I wouldn't be surprised if you were to see him again soon.

I'm enjoying my work. I'm convinced that my technique – and hence insight into the workings of the sick and healthy psyche – will take shape, as if by itself.

I get little joy out of my colleagues here, on the other hand there's nothing particularly embarrassing either. More likely indifference on my part. As regards family matters, I strive to attain some clarification – both internally as well as externally.

I know it's for me to make the first move by recognising certain essential things which every woman from the depths of her psychic make-up expects to be acknowledged. I refer of course to women's 'narcissistic' needs.

Such a pity you live so far away. It was marvellous having a friend around.

Somehow the air in Baden-Baden did more for the intimacy we share between us, though.[5]

Love to dear Emke, your faithful partner and comrade-in-arms. She made a great impression here, all round.

Your Sándor

---

[1] On 24th November 1925, the Groddecks paid a visit to Freud in Vienna shortly after one of his cancer-related operations. Freud was tired. The visit to Vienna was on the return to Baden-Baden from the Groddeck trip to Budapest. For their own words see Freud-Groddeck letters (*The Meaning of Illness*, p.94).

[2] Sándor Radó. See n.3, pp.45-6.

[3] 'It is tossed by the waves, but does not sink.' See Freud, 'On the history of the psychoanalytic movement', Collected Works, S.E., 14.

[4] Frédéric [Frigyes] Kovács (1882-1944), architect, and second husband of Vilma Kovács (1883-1940), Budapest psychoanalyst and close colleague and friend of Ferenczi. They are the grandparents of Judith Dupont – Ferenczi's literary executor.

[5] A reference to the nature of their contact on Groddeck's two-week visit with his wife to Budapest in November 1925. On 14th November Groddeck gave a lecture, 'Psychoanalytic Therapy of Internal Diseases', to the Hungarian Psychoanalytic Society. Ferenczi mentioned his visit in the *Rundbrief*, 28th November.

Sándor Ferenczi to Georg and Emmy Groddeck

Budapest, 7th January 1926

Dear Georg and Emke,

Since I last wrote, I have been in your country representing the Professor at Abraham's funeral.[1] In Berlin an analyst friend of A.'s [Abraham] told me that A. had removed himself almost in a state of fear from all analytic influence and had, so to speak, deliberately offered himself up to the lethal thrusts of the surgeon's knife. On top of it all, when he was practically in the throes of death he underwent what seems to have been a totally unnecessary laparotomy; on the following day, his stomach wound burst open during a coughing fit (detached retina, peritonitis).[2]

He was very popular in Berlin. Eitingon,[3] who will take over from him, will only be able to replace him on an administrative level. The Professor expressed the wish that I should move to Berlin;[4] some of the younger Berliners (Simmel,[5] Alexander[6]) seem supportive of this idea. These plans do not appeal to my unadventurous nature in the least.

Nothing much happening here. Over Christmas we were in Vienna, where the news of A.'s death caught up with me. My wife went back to Budapest, and I on to Berlin.

It was marvellous that we were able to see each other in the autumn, too, this time.[7] But you won't be able to get away with not seeing me in the summer this year – we are not going to make things that easy for you.

Sarolta is with us. We get the impression that she's physically and mentally much better than she was in Rome;[8] the situation

70

with the lawyer is obviously very unpleasant. She is unwilling to accept your invitation, and has no money herself. So, even though she would like nothing more than to visit you, she feels unable to allow herself this pleasure. Kovács,[9] too, can't or won't permit himself to take so much time away from home and off work. Perhaps he'll make do with asking for analytic help from Dr. Deutsch[10] in Vienna.

I'm avidly working on my cases, and am always learning something new. But the actual implementation of plans is still inhibited by pleasure anxiety (strictly speaking, reluctance and lethargy).

We are very pleased that you enjoyed yourselves here – and anticipate that having acquired a taste for the place, you will want to come again.

Thank you for the New Year telegram!

Your Sándor

[1] Karl Abraham (1877-1925), founder of the Berlin Psychoanalytic Society. Abraham died on Christmas day. In fact, Ferenczi was not supportive of Abraham's style and direction in psychoanalysis.

[2] Abraham seemingly died from lung cancer which was not diagnosed. Ferenczi is here referring to an operation Abraham had for what was thought to be gall-bladder trouble in October. (It is interesting to note that Wilhelm Fliess, Freud's former friend, was, at a point during this time, Abraham's doctor.)

[3] Max Eitingon was president of the International Psychoanalytic Association from 1925-1932.

[4] This becomes an issue for a period of time between Freud and Ferenczi. See *Freud-Ferenczi Correspondence*, 3rd and 18th January 1926 letters.

[5] Ernst Simmel (1882-1947), Berlin psychoanalyst and a founder of the Berlin Psychoanalytic Institute. Simmel opened a psychoanalytic sanatorium near Berlin called *Tegelsee* in which Freud took a great interest and at which he occasionally stayed. Simmel became a supporter of Groddeck (see his testimonial for Groddeck's 60th birthday in *Internationale Zeitschrift für Psychoanalyse* (1926), 12: pp.591-595).

[6] Franz Alexander (1891-1964), Hungarian psychoanalyst; trained with Sachs and

Abraham in Berlin. He liked Ferenczi's work and wrote a positive review of *Thalassa* and an important paper on Ferenczi's relaxation technique. Alexander emigrated to Chicago and is especially known for his contributions to brief psychotherapy and psychosomatic medicine, and, particularly in relation to Ferenczi's work, the concept of 'corrective emotional experience'. It is noteworthy that younger analysts such as Simmel and Alexander were very interested in psychosomatics.

[7] A reference to the Groddecks' Budapest visit, November 1925. See letter of 6th December 1925, n.5, p.69.

[8] Sarolta Morando, née Altschul, lived in Rome. See also n.3, p.28.

[9] Frédéric Kovács. See n.4, p.69, and Appendix 1.

[10] Probably Dr. Felix Deutsch. He was also a psychoanalyst who specialised in applying psychoanalysis to organically ill patients, and probably encouraged Ferenczi to consult Groddeck in the first place (*The Wild Analyst* and *The Meaning of Illness*).

[**Ed. comment**: On 13th March 1926 Ferenczi gave a lecture to the Hungarian Psychoanalytic Society: 'The problem of the acceptance of unpleasant ideas.']

Sándor Ferenczi to Georg and Emmy Groddeck

Budapest, 27th March 1926[1]

Dear Friends,

First some news:

1.) A few weeks ago Freud felt unwell: heart problems.[2] Dr. Lévy[3] of Budapest and Prof. Braun[4] (Vienna) referred him to the Cottage Sanatorium[5] where he made a good recovery, as he writes. Dr. Lévy says the problems are not serious.[6]

2.) Former students and patients of mine in America have prompted the 'New School for Social Research' to invite me for a series of lectures. I have accepted in principle, and providing I succeed in giving enough private sessions, I (viz: we) will cross the ocean at the end of September and stay over there for the whole of the autumn, winter and spring. We will be passing through Baden-Baden in September, and what is more, this time without patients. We would love to drop in and stay with you again, at least for a bit.

3.) Up to a short while ago, my health was unstable. Right now I seem to have hit upon the right dose of self-knowledge and other appropriate therapy.[7]

Now to you!

For goodness sake let's hear from you. We hear bits via *The Ark*,[8] but that's really not enough – far from it. I find something of interest in nearly every issue of *The Ark* – here and there even little barbs directed against analysts of my ilk and against little active ingenuities.[9]

How are Miss Collins and Mrs. Inman?[10] Dr. Inman[11] sent me New Year greetings, without, however, referring to his wife.

And how are you both? Have you already been to the little hut[12] in the wood?

I enclose the seeds from California which my wife promised you. I hope they flower in front of the little hut.

So – warm greetings and friendly kisses (or vice versa)

from your Sándor

---

[1] This letter was incorrectly dated as 6th March 1927 in earlier published editions.

[2] In mid-February 1926 Freud suffered mild attacks of angina pectoris. See *Freud-Ferenczi Correspondence*, Vol. III, p.251.

[3] Lajos Lévy (1875-1961), Hungarian physician and in 1913 founding member and treasurer of the Hungarian Psychoanalytic Association. He was Ferenczi's friend and personal physician and was consulted by Freud 1923-1928 (Schur, 1972, p.407).

[4] Professor Ludwig Braun (1881-1936). A well-known Viennese cardiologist, Freud's doctor and friend.

[5] Freud went to the Cottage Sanatorium 5th March, and stayed for about a month at

this immense and luxurious sanatorium founded in 1908 on the outskirts of Vienna. He referred to the sanatorium as 'my Riviera' (Schur, 1972, p.396).

[6] Ferenczi actually believed Freud's heart condition was psychological and offered to come to Vienna for a few months to analyse him. Freud turned him down. See *Freud-Ferenczi Correspondence*, 26th and 27th February, and 1st and 3rd March 1926.

[7] Ferenczi was constantly trying other methods of 'therapy' (E. Falzeder, personal communication, Feb. 1995).

[8] Sanatorium journal. See n.2, p.67.

[9] In German: 'aktiven Kunststückchen'. Possibly a reference to Groddeck's challenging Ferenczi about his 'active technique'.

[10] Two regular and longtime English patients at Groddeck's sanatorium. Mollie Collins, who died in 1956, was introduced to Groddeck at the 1925 Bad Homburg conference by Dr. William Inman. She had a neurological illness and was treated for a number of years by Groddeck. Collins was an enthusiastic supporter and translated some of his works into English. Mrs. Inman, wife of Dr. William Inman, became a patient of Groddeck's at about the same time. Their names regularly appear in the sanatorium guestbook.

[11] Dr. William S. Inman, British opthalmic surgeon, who claimed that the majority of patients who consult an opthamologist are emotionally disturbed. He was analysed in the 1920s by Ferenczi, who introduced Inman to Groddeck. Inman regularly came to Baden-Baden when Ferenczi was there to continue his analysis, and came to admire Groddeck (*The Wild Analyst*).

[12] See p.60, n.1.

Sándor Ferenczi to Georg Groddeck

Budapest, 26th June 1926

Dear Friend,

It's been a long time since I last wrote to you. In the meantime I have been put under tremendous pressure to give up the trip to America and to move to Vienna to take over the chairmanship. It was Prof. Freud who particularly argued <u>for</u> Vienna and <u>against</u> America.[1] I was in two minds for ages, but finally decided to go ahead with the American plan after all. There is no chance of my making <u>much</u> money over there, but even so I hope to consolidate my connections abroad.[2] I don't yet know what I will be doing after that.

We <u>definitely</u> intend to travel via Baden-Baden to Paris and on to the French port where we are to embark. Greatly looking forward to being with you again. We should arrive towards the end of August, or – more likely – beginning of September.

We are at present staying in a pension near Budapest until mid-August (Address: <u>Budapest, I. Martonhegyi ut. 45, Villa Montana</u>). Rotten weather – yet it's nicer here than being in the dark apartment in Nagydiófa u.3.[3]

Affectionate greetings from us both to you and dear Emke,

Your Sándor

---

[1] It seems that Freud and the other Committee members had concerns about Ferenczi's trip to America; for example, that he might decide to stay there; or that there would be a negative influence on him, as had been interpreted in Jung's and Rank's case. Rank had recently left Vienna and appeared to be settling in America. See *Freud-Ferenczi Correspondence*, 23rd April 1926.

[2] Ferenczi had an increasing number of patients from the United States.

[3] Martonhegyi utca is in the hills on the Buda side of the Danube. The Ferenczis' apartment on Nagydiófa utca, where they lived until 1930, was in the busy, more commercial Pest side, just off the bustling main street, Rakoczi utca.

Sándor and Gizella Ferenczi to Georg Groddeck

Budapest, 26th July 1926

Dear Georg,

It seems ever more likely that we shall stay about 8 days on the Semmering,[1] and just as long again in Munich, where I intend having a detailed discussion with Lou Salomé, as well as a few days in the mountains. So we will be with you around 6th-8th

September and stay for about 8-10 days. We haven't yet decided on the subsequent route to the port (Hamburg or Cherbourg), which will depend on the political situation in Paris.[2]

Kindest greetings to you all from

the Ferenczis

[1] Visiting Freud. See n.5, p.59.
[2] Probably a reference to the trouble over the collapse of the French franc, and Poincaré's recall to the presidency, supported by the large banking interests attempting to restore the franc. This trouble, although relatively moderate, was enough to scare those who had recently experienced the inflation in Central Europe.

Sándor and Gizella Ferenczi to Georg and Emmy Groddeck

Munich, 30th August 1926

Dear Friends,

We celebrated Gizella's birthday here in Munich, where we met up with Frau Lou Salomé, and before that we spent a week on the Semmering with Prof. Freud.[1] We shall <u>almost</u> certainly bring Frau Salomé with us to Baden-Baden as our guest; she will probably stay 2-3 days. We are not sure yet when we shall be arriving, although it could be as early as this Thursday. We will definitely send you a telegram.[2] We are <u>very much</u> looking forward to seeing you so soon. Please let my sister-in-law know we're coming, if she is still with you.[3]

Fondly,

Your Sándor

and Gizella

P.S. If at all possible please reserve rooms for us and Frau Salomé at the Marienhöhe; if there is no room for Frau Lou, we would like to put her up in the immediate vicinity.

S.

---

[1] Beginning 22nd/23rd August, the Ferenczis stayed in a hotel (probably the 'Süd-bahnhotel') near the villa where Freud was holidaying (*Freud-Ferenczi Correspondence*, 25th July 1926).

[2] The Ferenczis, along with Lou Salomé, arrived at the sanatorium Thursday, 2nd September. Lou Salomé left four days later, on the 6th, and the Ferenczis left for France on 18th September. The Ferenczis sailed for New York on 23rd September 1926 on the *Andania* (Cunard line) from Cherbourg, France.

[3] Sarolta Morando. She was at Groddeck's sanatorium for two months from late July until late September 1926. It is interesting to note that Walter Schmideberg, husband of Melanie Klein's daughter Melitta Schmideberg, was also at the sanatorium at this time (see also Appendix 1, p.126).

Sándor Ferenczi to Georg Groddeck

Still in Baden-Baden,

for the 13th October 1926[1]

Dear Georg Groddeck,

I congratulate you with all my heart on the 60th anniversary of your birthday. Looking back on the history of our friendship on this occasion, I can see that it had initially a purely scientific, impersonal basis and began as a correspondence between you, Freud and myself about how psychoanalysis can be applied in organic medicine.[2] Then, later on, I got to know you as a physician and human being when I myself became ill organically, since when no year has passed without some weeks of rest,

77

regeneration and exchange of confidences in the intimacy of your home in Baden-Baden. There are decided differences between us with regard to the scientific method we employ; yet we always managed to bridge these outward differences with a bit of goodwill on both our parts and essentially to harmonise our views. I have learned a lot from the carefree courage with which you 'come to grips' with the psychomorphology of the organic, but flatter myself that I have had some influence on your development too. Psychoanalysis has undoubtedly received significant impulses from you; the best in our profession know this only too well, even if they somewhat begrudge you your rights to priority in current psychoanalytic writing.[3] As you appear not to care excessively about matters of priority, you're not particularly bothered by being neglected like this.[4] You can rest assured that your friends and patients appreciate you.

Best wishes till the next anniversary

from your Sándor Ferenczi

[1] This letter for Groddeck's 60th birthday was written by Ferenczi before he left for North America.

[2] It is interesting that Ferenczi frames the beginning of their friendship as a triangle which includes Freud. Indeed, Freud sent the first letter he received from Groddeck to Ferenczi for advice (Dr. Judith Dupont, personal communication, April 1995). See 'Freud-Groddeck Correspondence' in *The Meaning of Illness*, and *Freud-Ferenczi Correspondence*, Vol. II, pp.212-13, and pp.217-18.

[3] Ferenczi (1925) defends Groddeck's intellectual priority in his paper – 'Contraindications to the "active" psycho-analytical technique', *Further Contributions to the Theory and Technique of Psycho-Analysis* (see p.225).

[4] Ferenczi's comment is ironic since he later runs into his own problems with Groddeck about his priority over intellectual property. (See Groddeck's letter of 13th June 1929, p.87, and Ferenczi's letters in response.)

Sándor Ferenczi to Georg and Emmy Groddeck

HOTEL ST. ANDREW

BROADWAY AT 72ND STREET

NEW YORK

New York, 26th April 1927[1]

Dear Georg and Emmy,

Gizella has gone to visit her sister (Mrs. Morando)[2] in Los Angeles; she's been away almost three weeks. I'm finishing my current work here in mid May, and will only meet latest, outstanding commitments – trip to Washington, etc;[3] we will leave here – sail – on 2nd June (boat *New York* of the Hamburg-America Line), arriving in London[4] about 10th June and intend – after a short stay in Paris – getting to <u>Baden-Baden</u> sometime between 20th-25th June, assuming you are able to fit us in.[5]

My intention is to rest for about three weeks and then to resume work whilst staying with you in Baden-Baden.

I can't wait to see you both again and to tell you all about my – pretty wild – American campaign.

I never fail to mention and praise Georg in my lectures as the standard bearer of psychoanalysis *in organicis*.

There are a few things I could say about my state of health – but I'll wait till I'm with you. On the whole: I cope!

The fruits of my visit *in toto*: about 2-2½ times more income than I would have made at home, numerous 'honours', and a certain success in promoting the cause of psychoanalysis. – I worked unbelievably hard in this respect – am exhausted.

79

My final task is to try to collect money for the publishing company.[6] I cannot imagine I'll succeed.

Very best wishes! I long for the peace I find with you,

Sándor

---

[1] Ferenczi misdates letter as 1926, when in fact he was in America from 3rd October 1926 to 2nd June 1927.
[2] Sarolta Morando. This name, as with other family names, did not appear in the earlier published editions. Gizella returned 10th-15th May 1927 (see *Freud-Ferenczi Correspondence*, letters of 8th April 1927, and 1st May 1927).
[3] In Washington, Ferenczi gave a talk at the St. Elizabeth's Asylum.
[4] Ferenczi landed in Southampton and went up to London where he gave talks, including his 1926 paper, 'Gulliver Phantasies' (Ferenczi, 1926a).
[5] Ferenczi signed into the sanatorium guestbook on 26th June and signed out on 28th August. Strangely, Gizella had not signed in as well. However there is no indication of any separation of the Ferenczis on this trip.
[6] The psychoanalytic press was in financial trouble.

Sándor Ferenczi to Georg and Emmy Groddeck

Dr. Ferenczi Sándor[1]

25th October 1927

Dear Pat and Patin,[2]

We were so happy to get your news, which exudes a spirit of wonderful harmony and contentment as always, despite the occasional trouble life throws at us. Indeed, I wouldn't have much to complain about – if it weren't for the dilemma Vienna/Budapest, which is still not quite sorted out and won't quite permit calm to descend.[3] Socially and politically things remain unstable here, even though the situation has improved considerably during our absence.[4] It is indeed tragic when aspersions are suddenly cast on one's national affiliations[5] after fifty years of 'belonging' to a country emotionally and spiritually. But for this, I would have opted for Budapest without hesitation.

I don't work much now – 5-6 hours daily; yet contrary to all expectation, I do nothing in my spare time – just loaf about.

It's funny how I have extricated myself so completely and so quickly from America. It all just seems like a dream now.

Every now and again, dear Pat, I put someone sick in touch with you, though you know how rarely 'they reach him!'

Elma is in Rome, staying with Sarolta. Zsuka is a hard-working journalist; they are beginning to appreciate her; little Erdös is already a doctor of law.

My wife wants me to leave her some space to write in, so I will close now and greet you both most warmly,

Your Sándor

I have got enough space – my dears – to embrace you warmly – and reassure you again and again of my devotion. Also best wishes once more for the recent and coming birthday – to both of you good fortune in equal measure – and the ability to enjoy life.

I'm happy to be with my loved ones again – which is hardly surprising after such a long absence. I'm surrounded by fine, good people – and feel bound to them. Miss Thau was so kind as to send me the pattern-book and to enclose a Swedish song for Sándor – I would like to thank her quickly but have no address – Sándor lost it. Please let me have it as soon as possible. I remain your loving and faithful Gizella.   27th October.

¹ It is Hungarian usage to put the surname first.
² 'Patin' is the female form of 'Pat', Groddeck's nickname. It also means 'godmother' in German.
³ See letter 26th June 1926, p.74, regarding pressures on Ferenczi to move to Vienna.
⁴ A reference to the continuing anti-Semitism in Hungary under Miklós Horthy's regime – a combination of traditional conservatism and right-wing radicalism. Horthy seized power from Béla Kun's communist government in 1919-1920. The Horthy regime gave rise to a violent anti-communist and anti-Semitic period known as the 'White terror'. Ferenczi was stripped of his short-lived professorship of psychoanalysis (1919), and was thrown out of the Hungarian Medical Society.
⁵ In a letter to Freud on 28th August 1919, Ferenczi wrote: 'We Hungarian Jews are now facing a period of brutal persecution of Jews. They will, I think, have cured us in a very short time of the illusion with which we were brought up, namely that we are "Hungarians of the Jewish faith" '.

Sándor Ferenczi to Georg and Emmy Groddeck¹

Budapest, 27th July 1928

Dear Friends,

How can I thank you for your kindness! Probably by declaring that I could not possibly be worthy of your goodness; anyway, I lack all powers of expression. So let's move on.

Enjoying parties, giving and receiving with grace are always a speciality of the Marienhöhe. Things were otherwise in Budapest. There was an official dinner in a restaurant, without any real atmosphere. Members of our group didn't manage to say a friendly word to me, or to squeeze one out of me. I was glad when the whole thing was over.²

A particularly difficult case³ that couldn't follow me to Germany was the main obstacle to our visiting you this time.⁴ Possibly also an intimation of that process of 'discarding' to which you allude, and which I perhaps do not wish to interrupt. I believe also that my own ideas are changing, and it is questionable whether we concur at every point in our views at present. Be that as it may: as individuals we will always remain close. I think that we recognise the sincerity of each other's aims.

For the moment our plan is to go to Spain[5] in the autumn. Wouldn't it be lovely if we could somehow co-ordinate our plans, or are you of the opinion, dear Georg, that we should go our own separate ways for the time being? Sometimes I have half a mind to find a place of peace and quiet where I can collect my thoughts on certain things that occupy me.

Dear Emke's lines display that irrepressible jollity and enthusiasm which we love so much in her. Reading her letter brought up the charming picture of your home and little hut so vividly for a moment.

We send kindest greetings to you and all our dear friends,

Your

Sándor

[1] First typed letter. All letters except four are handwritten.

[2] Probably a reference to a disappointing celebration of Ferenczi's 55th birthday in Budapest.

[3] The 'difficult case' was Elizabeth Severn (1879-1959), an American 'psychotherapist', patient and pupil of Ferenczi's, later code-named in his diary as 'R.N.' Severn worked with Ferenczi from 1924 until a few months before his death in 1933. Severn had had a major breakthrough in her treatment earlier in 1928, which had left her somewhat desperate emotionally, and psychologically dependent on Ferenczi. Obviously Ferenczi didn't want to interrupt her treatment at this critical point. Although little known, she was an important influence on Ferenczi in his last years, and initiated Ferenczi's experiment in mutual analysis (Ferenczi, 1932). Ferenczi acknowledged her influence in two of his last papers 'The principle of relaxation and neocatharsis', (1930b), pp.121-22, and 'Child analysis in the analysis of adults', (1931), pp.133-34, *Final Contributions to the Problems and Methods of Psycho-Analysis*. As the case of 'R.N.', Severn played a large role in Ferenczi's *Clinical Diary* (1932). For more on Severn and Ferenczi, see Fortune (1993) 'The Case of "RN": Sándor Ferenczi's radical experiment in psychoanalysis.' See also Fortune (1994), and (1996).

[4] 1928 was a critical point in Ferenczi's work with Severn (Fortune, 1993). Ferenczi, as can be seen by a later statement to Groddeck, is starting to feel that Severn's case is not only a critically important development in his own work, but that he must see it through as it may be a key to a new development in psychoanalysis, *vis-à-vis* his work with technique and now trauma.

[5] The Ferenczis left for Spain on 30th September, and the trip included Madrid, Sevilla, and Granada. Elizabeth Severn accompanied them.

Sándor and Gizella Ferenczi to Georg and Emmy Groddeck

Granada, Hotel Casino,
Alhambra Palace
17th October 1928

Dear Friends,

We couldn't even congratulate Pat on his birthday – not having any idea where you were! So: all the very best for the future! May the Doctor retain his eternal youth for the delectation of all around him. I await with curiosity and interest the results of his latest ideas.

I'm in Spain taking a break. You must come here some time: the atmosphere, the colours, people, antiquities are beyond compare. Freud's translator in Madrid wants me to give a lecture (on the return journey). I will give it in French and he will translate it into Spanish.[1]

As for the physicians here, they are half still Breuerian,[2] half already Jungian, without ever having been Freudian.

I'm starting again on the 5th in Budapest.

Best wishes,
Your Sándor

84

Dear Groddecks – Many thanks for your congratulations for August 30th – which I return with all my heart, dearest Doctor. We thought of you a lot on the 13th – and were sorry that we couldn't get in touch. What a pity that you didn't want to come with us. I embrace you in loving friendship,

Your Gizella

---

[1] Besides Hungarian, Ferenczi spoke German, English and French.

[2] Influenced by Joseph Breuer (1842-1925), Viennese physiologist and internist, whom Freud credited with playing a critical part in the development of psychoananlysis. He was a pioneer in the use of hypnotism in the cathartic treatment of hysteria, a method which formed the basis for his collaboration with Freud in the early 1890s and led to their joint publication, *Studies on Hysteria* (1895).

Sándor Ferenczi to Georg Groddeck

Budapest, 12th February 1929

Dear Friend,

The enclosed letter should serve to clarify the telegram[1] I sent you yesterday. As well as putting my signature to the content of Frau von Tésrey's lines, or rather, requesting that the wish contained therein be met (if possible), I would add that Fr. v. T. is an exceptionally intelligent and morally upright lady, the widow of our Fine Arts Museum director, and is herself an outstanding journalist. (She writes for the *Frankfurter Zeitung*, *Pester Lloyd*, *New York Times*, etc.)

I'm not feeling too bad. I cope with my symptoms and little aches and pains in various ways – trying this, trying that. Overall: so-so!

I'm making perceptible strides in understanding the nature of neuroses – with not inconsiderable benefits for therapy. Perhaps I can make the effort to share these insights with others one day.[2]

I hear little of Association[3] proceedings. I was in Vienna for a day last week. The Prof. is feeling <u>much</u> better since they adjusted his prosthesis[4] in Berlin. He wants to get down to work again.

How did you get on in England?[5] And in Berlin?

Do write to us when you get the chance. We think of you so very often.

Your

Sándor

[1] Telegram not preserved.

[2] Ferenczi was aware that this work with recovered memories of early trauma would not be met with favour by most of the psychoanalytic community, including Freud.

[3] The International Psychoanalytic Association.

[4] Over the years Freud was constantly bothered by his wooden jaw prosthesis which necessitated a number of different versions and many adjustments to the fit.

[5] Groddeck (1929) had presented a paper, 'Psychical treatment of organic disease', to the Medical Section of the British Psychological Society on 28th November 1928. He visited England again in August 1930, giving a paper at the Congress for Sex Research in London: 'Organic affection specialised as a form of sexual expression'. This last paper, more directed towards general psychotherapy than psychoanalysis, suggests Groddeck was moving in the direction of the broader scope of 'psychotherapy'.

Georg Groddeck to Sándor Ferenczi

DR. MED. G. GRODDECK
BADEN-BADEN, WERDERSTR. 14

13th June 1929

Dear Sándor,

Quite by chance, or – to be more specific – it was my bookseller who told me about your arbitary jump from the psychic to the organic,[1] and now I'm not sure I know what to do about you. Perhaps you can sort this out; it would be good for both of us.

In the first place, there is no question of it having been an arbitary jump: it was I who introduced you very gently and carefully to these ideas. Such caution was necessary since you yourself had told me how you reacted to my first communications with Freud.[2] If I was to get anywhere with you I would have to proceed very gently.

Secondly, I want to reclaim my property,[3] not that I ever considered this property a personal discovery. That would have meant destroying my knowledge of long-predeceased thinkers, and I would never have succeeded, because I know an awful lot about their work. But it is none the less my property, because I acquired it in the course of years of work. You can of course claim originality in your skilful arrangement of the wording, for no one else can lay claim to the Genital Theory[4] nor the ghastly expression 'Bioanalysis' – but this does not apply to the rest.

I realise that it is not easy in this case to beat a retreat. But it is essential that you do so. Think about it! – We're not going to Oxford.[5]

In old friendship, and with kindest greetings from us both
to you and yours[6]

[1] Probably a reference to Ferenczi's shift in theoretical and clinical emphasis as expressed
in his 1929 paper 'Masculine and feminine,' *The Psychoanalytic Review*, 1930, 17,
pp.105-113. In it Ferenczi wrote: 'I have simply transferred purely psychological
conceptions such as repression and symbol formation to organic processes, but I am
not at all certain that this bold leap from the psychic to the organic was really only an
error and not rather a successful coup: a discovery. I believe the latter, and regard these
ideas as the beginning of a new method of investigation... "Bioanalysis"' (p.109).
See, however, the authorised translation of *Thalassa: A Theory of Genitality*, p.102
(reprinted London: Karnac, 1989), where 'bold leap' is translated as 'arbitary jump'.
[2] Initially, Ferenczi was suspicious of Groddeck's 'mysticism'.
[3] Namely, Groddeck's original work championing the application of psychoanalysis
to organic illness, and the exploration of the psycho-physical relationship.
[4] *Thalassa: A Theory of Genitality*.
[5] The 11th Congress of the International Psycho-Analytical Association was held in
Oxford, England, 27th-31st July 1929. At the Congress, six weeks after Groddeck's
critical letter, Ferenczi presented his paper 'Progresses in psycho-analytic technique'
(later expanded and published as 'The principle of relaxation and neocatharsis,' (1930b),
Final Contributions to the Problems and Methods of Psycho-Analysis, pp.108-125.
In his paper, Ferenczi made a diplomatic gesture to credit Groddeck's influence. He
wrote:

> The relaxation-technique which I am suggesting to you assuredly obliterates
> even more completely the distinction between the analysis of children and that
> of adults – a distinction hitherto too sharply drawn. In making the two types of
> treatment more like one another I was undoubtedly influenced by what I saw of
> the work of Georg Groddeck, the courageous champion of the psycho-analysis
> of organic diseases, whom I consulted about an organic illness. I felt that he was
> right in trying to encourage his patients to a childlike naiveté, and I saw the
> success thus achieved... (pp.122-123).

At the same time, however, Ferenczi did not capitulate to Groddeck's demands to
retreat, since in the last part of the paragraph he attempts to define his own new path
(which also held to Freud's ideas): 'But, for my own part, I have remained faithful to
the well-tried analytical method of frustration as well, and I try to attain my aim by the
tactful and understanding application of *both* forms of technique' (p.123).
[6] Groddeck did not sign the letter.

Sándor Ferenczi to Georg Groddeck

St. Moritz Village (Switzerland), Hotel Schweizerhof
7th July 1929

Dear Friend,

The above date[1] prompts me to assure you and Emke of my unchanged tender feelings.

My telegram and request for immediate clarification referred to the part which – having been pointed out by your bookseller – reminded you of your authorship rights. I should be grateful if you would reply. Indeed, I would like detailed information about <u>every</u> reproach so that I am in a position to check the material, and – if my conscience should demand it (and insofar as it compels me) – grant you satisfaction.

I'm working here, instead of in Budapest, having remembered last year's tropical Hungarian heat, but have instead encountered unusually cold weather, though also a lot of sunshine.

With kind regards from house to house,

Your

Sándor

---

[1] Ferenczi's birthday, 7th July. In 1929, Ferenczi turned 56 years old.

Sándor Ferenczi to Georg Groddeck

SCHWEIZERHOF – HOTEL SUISSE
ST. MORITZ-DORF

St. Moritz, 16th August 1929

Dear Friend,

Although you have refused to discuss further certain mis-understandings[1] between us which I continue to find totally incomprehensible I see no reason for breaking off our friendly relationship.

I have a question for you today or rather, a request:

I have been here in St. Moritz (Hotel Schweizerhof) since July,[2] as usual with patients and students[3] whom I didn't want to treat in the intense heat of Budapest. The trouble is that I can't get on with the altitude[4] here. My heart problems frequently bring on those early morning breathing difficulties, etc. Naturally I think about visiting you again and having a rest. So may I ask you to fit us in somewhere, where I can also work (as before). I'd also like to put up one of my pupils, whom you know (Severn), in your house if possible, because she is at a critical stage.

I am counting on you to tell me in your usual forthright manner whether this plan suits you, or whether you would prefer me to work outside the sanatorium precincts (which I would find acceptable even though it would not be as convenient for me as on previous visits).[5]

With best wishes from Gizella and myself to you and Emke,

Your old Sándor Ferenczi

90

P.S. We are hoping for a reply by return of post as to whether this plan for the end of August or beginning of September is feasible. Another possibility would be a little room nearby to work in, and a sitting-room in your house.

[1] See Groddeck's letter of 13th June 1929, p.87, which initiated an exchange of letters dealing with Groddeck's charge that Ferenczi misappropriated his intellectual 'property' – the psychoanalysis of organically-based symptoms.

[2] Ferenczi stayed in St. Moritz from early July to late August.

[3] Among these were a number of notable Americans including Elizabeth Severn, Clara Thompson, MD (1893-1958) and Izette de Forest – patients mentioned by code-name in Ferenczi's *Clinical Diary*. The best known was Clara Thompson, who worked with Ferenczi during the summers from 1928 until his death in 1933. She co-founded the William Alanson White Institute in New York with Harry Stack Sullivan (1892-1949) and Erich Fromm (1900-1980). Izette de Forest, a lay analyst, wrote of Ferenczi's work in *The Leaven of Love* (New York: Da Capo Press, 1954). According to psychoanalyst Dr. Clifford Scott, who saw Melanie Klein for analytical sessions during her holiday in the early 1930s, the practice of continuing analysis while on holiday, or in retreat settings such as sanatoriums or resorts, during the summer months was not unusual in those days (C. Scott, personal communication, 6th April 1991).

[4] St. Moritz elevation: 1,856 metres (6,089 feet).

[5] Groddeck obviously made room for the Ferenczis, as Sándor and Gizella signed their arrival and departure dates into the sanatorium guestbook: '27/VIII to 27/X' (two months).

Sándor Ferenczi to Georg and Emmy Groddeck

Monday, 28th October 1929

Dear Pat and Emke,

Many thanks again for everything! This year it really was a 'relaxation'[1] for me – thanks to you!

91

The journey back went off all right – even the Gr.[2] tried hard not to be unpleasant. We arrived without coming to blows. The family was waiting at home. It was all very homely. They all asked after you – particularly Zsuka. Elma will be coming in two to three days' time.

I'm afraid that my patients (the regular ones) are determined to swamp me; hardly one of them is prepared to interrupt the treatment. Accepting new ones is out of the question.[3]

I want to hand all responsibility for Association business over to the younger members.[4]

Enclosed are the few marks I still owe Fräulein Spalding.

Our love to the hut,[5] the house, and all the inhabitants of your island realm.

With a kiss for Emke's hand, as well as sending the usual kisses,

Sándor

[1] Ferenczi's use of the word 'relaxation' in this way is probably also a play on the name he has given to a new aspect of his clinical method, the 'relaxation technique' which he presented to the Oxford Congress in July (Ferenczi, 1930b). See also n.5, p.88.

[2] 'Gr.' is short for 'Gräfin' – 'Countess' in this instance, and refers to Elizabeth Severn, because Ferenczi later (20th March 1933) uses the whole word 'Gräfin' to denote her. Severn was living in Budapest at this time and, given her critical condition, quite likely would have travelled back to Budapest from Baden-Baden with the Ferenczis. See above, p.90, letter 16th August 1929.

[3] Since Ferenczi was often referred the most difficult patients, his caseload was by now heavy with these, often long-term, cases.

[4] Ferenczi is probably referring to the Hungarian Psychoanalytic Association.

[5] See n.1, p.60.

Sándor Ferenczi to Georg and Emmy Groddeck

Budapest, 15th June 1930

Dear Pat and Patin,

The laziest letter-writer in the world has decided after all to show signs of life.[1] Oh, if only it were true this matter of thought transference![2] Then you would already be well-informed about everything, would know how often we think of you, and speak of you.

Follows a short report on the passed or currently passing year *quoad me*:

Almost without exception bad nights with accompanying headaches and breathing problems. After countless attempts at finding alleviation I may have succeeded – so that I feel a little better now.

Now for the real news: we have bought a villa, consisting of two floors with garden, over on the Ofner hill[3] and will be moving in towards the end of this month. So we have become homeowners at the same time as you. Another apartment on the first floor will be let. It was a good buy (for approximately 70,000 Marks) but the necessary alterations will be rather expensive (around 30,000!). I look forward to getting fresh air and sun, which I greatly missed here.[4] Perhaps I can go on living for a while after all.

With regard to intellectual progress, it's been a very successful year. My thoughts are beginning to crystallise around specific themes; a book will eventually materialise,[5] I certainly know much more than before.

We won't be going on holiday till October; perhaps we will bump into you somewhere – or end up coming to you again?[6]

It always makes us happy to see Emke's handwriting. Nobody writes so sweetly and so vividly.

As ever in devoted friendship,

Your Sándor

P.S.

I have just come back from the Kovácses. Herr K. is not that well; his symptoms are troubling him again. I advised him to contact you again,[7] and offered to write to you, or rather (upon his wish) enquire if you would advise resumption of his treatment. I know, of course, what you are wont to say under such circumstances ('Come, if you feel like it'), but I am keeping my promise – hence this note. I am sure a stay with you would once again do him good. Please have another look at him and let me know by return of post if there is a vacancy for him, and if so, when.[8]

Best wishes

S.

[1] There seems to have been a gap of almost eight months in their correspondence.

[2] Ferenczi had a long-standing interest in telepathy; while sympathetic to the possibility – he participated in thought transference experiments with Freud and Anna Freud – he still remained to be convinced by scientific evidence (Ferenczi, 1932, p.33, and p.85). Ferenczi had delivered a lecture on thought transference to the Vienna Psycho-Analytical Association, 19th November 1913. At this time during the 1920s and early 1930s, Ferenczi was also being exposed to the strongly-held ideas of thought transference by his analysand, Elizabeth Severn (Ferenczi, 1932, p.158). See also Fortune (1993, p.115), and n.26, p.18.

[3] Specifically, a neighbourhood called Naphegy ('Sun hill'), one of the hills on the Buda side of Budapest, on the north side and overlooking the Danube. The Ferenczis' villa was at 11 Lisznyai Street near the top of Naphegy, and perpendicular to Orvos (Doctor) Street, where Frédéric and Vilma Kovács lived. A small number of the close

Hungarian analysts lived here. At the bottom of the hill, a ten-minute walk, at 12 Meszaros Street, the first psychoanalytic clinic was opened in a house where Michael and Alice Balint lived, which was owned and built by the Kovács. Ferenczi's house, which was greatly damaged during the war, has been reconstructed, and in 1983 a plaque commemorating the 50th anniversary of his death was placed on the outside stone wall facing Lisznyai Street.

[4] The dark apartment of 3 Nagydiófa Street in a busy section of downtown Pest, just one street off Rákóczi Street.

[5] Ferenczi never did write a book on these themes. However, he published a number of his most important papers between 1930 and 1933 (Ferenczi, 1930b, 1931, 1933). He also wrote many notes during this period which were published posthumously as 'Notes and fragments' (1930-32), as well as his important *Clinical Diary* (1932). Elizabeth Severn claimed that she and Ferenczi had planned to write a book together about their clinical work; instead she published her own book (Severn, 1933) in the autumn shortly after Ferenczi's death.

[6] The Ferenczis did end up in Baden-Baden at the sanatorium, 2nd-14th October (sanatorium guestbook).

[7] Frédéric Kovács was treated by Groddeck in early 1927; his stay is recorded as 6th January-3rd March 1927 in the sanatorium guestbook. See Appendix 1.

[8] It is not clear whether Kovács returned to Groddeck for treatment. The sanatorium guestbook shows no entry for him in 1930 or 1931. Judith Dupont thinks there was more than one visit (personal communication, May 1995).

Sándor Ferenczi to Georg and Emmy Groddeck

BUDAPEST, I. LISZNYAI U.11

TELEPHONE: 573-87

21st December 1930

Dear Pat and Emke,

As I'm in a mood for writing, which usually doesn't last long, I'll get my Christmas greetings off to you. Emke's vivid and detailed accounts of your various houses and their inhabitants provide that feeling of continuity which was so abruptly curtailed by our sudden departure.[1] It seems to us as if we are personally present at all your birthday parties,[2] as if we were listening with

95

rapt attention to Pat's interesting lectures[3] and to Emke's gently mocking, 'impossible' and enthusiastic stories. I hope you find my wife's replies ample compensation for my persistent silence.

The trip to Vienna did me good. The differences of opinion turned out to be relatively superficial; on the contrary, I encountered pronounced co-operation compared to previous altercations.[4]

I am deeply engrossed – I should say up to my neck in work; I find increasing confirmation and verification of my ideas,[5] but am so exhausted after work that I am still unable to give them written formulation. Nor have I learned how to sleep yet; only very recently have things begun to improve in this respect.

Interest is growing for the Association,[6] which lay fallow for so long. The proposed plan in certain influential quarters[7] to make me president is beginning to interest me.[8]

I was very happy to hear that the Berliners have got as far as wanting to listen to you, dear Pat. I would be pleased if both of you would enlarge a bit on the apparently somewhat intricate personal conflicts among the Berliners.[9]

I have to devote four, sometimes nearly five hours daily to my main patient, 'the Queen'.[10] Hard work, but rewarding. I think I will soon – or in the not too distant future – be able to say what it means to finish an analysis.[11] The other patients are busily enacting[12] as well, and confirm daily what I wrote about the need to give due recognition again to traumatogenesis. Analysis, though, as I practise it, demands far greater self-sacrifice than was hitherto the case with us.[13]

But enough of talking shop. It's Sunday today; it's sunny, bracingly cold, the small garden a playground for finches, black-

96

birds, woodpeckers, crows and sparrows, drawn by the good food hung out everywhere. On days like this even I stop moaning and groaning, and my first step on leaving this mood is to write this letter.[14]

In anticipation of your, I hope, good news, greetings from

Your Sándor

---

[1] Seemingly a reference to the Ferenczi's last sanatorium visit which concluded after twelve days on 14th October.

[2] See n.6, p.42.

[3] Groddeck regularly gave extempore lectures and talked about dreams at the sanatorium.

[4] Ferenczi visited Freud in Vienna on 12th-13th April 1930 and discussed the direction of his clinical work (Ferenczi to Freud, 30th April 1930). Differences had been growing between them on technical and theoretical issues since the mid-1920s. Their letters through the late 1920s and early 1930s chronicle the growing strain this placed on their relationship.

[5] Ferenczi was becoming convinced that psychoanalysis was 'overestimating the role of fantasy, and underestimating that of traumatic reality, in pathogenesis' (Ferenczi to Freud, 25th December 1929, cited in *Clinical Diary*, p.xii).

[6] International Psychoanalytic Association.

[7] Freud.

[8] Ferenczi had an on-again, off-again interest in taking on the presidency of the IPA at this time. Freud seemed to be using the idea of the presidency to coax Ferenczi out of his growing isolation in Budapest. Ferenczi was tempted, but finally rejected the idea in a letter to Freud, 21st August 1932, cited in *Clinical Diary*, p.xvi.

[9] The Berlin Psychoanalytic Society, of which Groddeck was a member. There were tensions and competition between the Berlin Institute and the Budapest analytical group; for example, Ferenczi criticised the Berlin group for their emphasis on theory over technique.

[10] Elizabeth Severn.

[11] Severn was Ferenczi's most demanding and difficult patient. Driven by what Freud called his 'furor sanandi' (rage to cure), Ferenczi was regularly seeing her twice a day, as well as at weekends and, if necessary, at night. Ferenczi's statement here confirms that Severn is central to his developing technical and theoretical ideas which led to his challenge to Freud and his reconsideration of a theory of trauma.

[12] Strachey's translation of 'agieren' as 'acting out' is presently being challenged by Hoffer (1996), who prefers 'enact' or 'enactment'.

[13] Ferenczi's attempt to cure – a 'healing through love' – seemed to involve, at great physical and mental cost to himself, an endless reaching out to patients. In his *Clinical Diary* (1932) and his last papers, particularly 'Confusion of tongues between adults

and the child' (1933), Ferenczi criticized the neutrality, abstinence, and authority of classical technique as re-abusive to patients, in some cases at the level of the 'basic fault' (Balint, 1968).
[14] Letter is typed.

Sándor Ferenczi to Georg Groddeck

Capri, Hotel Quisisana,
10th October 1931

Dear Friend,

Most affectionate greetings from this delightful land. What a pity that I cannot congratulate you[1] here in this sun and sea spa. Don't fail to come here when you have collected enough pounds sterling.[2] It's so beautiful! – and no more expensive than Germany.

I am really trying to recover after all the extreme mental and physical exhaustion.[3] This time – for the first time in years – I have gone on holiday without patients.[4] –

Quoad science: I am grappling with the problem of <u>the trauma</u> as such: the splitting,[5] indeed, atomisation of the personality invites a stimulating if most complicated game of riddle solving, which brings you perilously close to the problem of death. (Mentally ill people are really half-dead persons).[6]

Gizella wants to congratulate you as well, so I will close with a salutation for you, Emke and all friends.

Your Sándor

Naturally I want to congratulate you too – dear Pat – and wish you all the very best. My dearest wish today would be to have you both here and to enjoy all this splendour with you. We have

98

no idea where our congratulations will reach you – in Baden-Baden? Or are you already *en route*? Please let us know – Hotel Quisisana, Capri. I embrace you both,

Your Gizella

[1] Ferenczi is no doubt referring to Groddeck's birthday on the 13th of October.

[2] Probably an allusion to Groddeck having British patients at the sanatorium. They had given him reputation and fame in England, which had resulted in several visits to Britain.

[3] Fatigue seems to be one of the early symptoms prefiguring Ferenczi's pernicious anaemia in the autumn of 1932, and from which he would die in May 1933.

[4] This same day, 10th October 1931 Ferenczi writes to Freud that he has wanted to have a holiday without patients for years.

[5] In his 1930 paper 'The principle of relaxation and neocatharsis' Ferenczi credits Elizabeth Severn's 'discoveries' for his understanding of this notion of splitting (*Final Contributions to the Problems and Methods of Psycho-Analysis*, pp.121-122).

[6] For further thoughts on this process and its relationship to death see *Clinical Diary*, particularly pp.8-10 (Case of R.N.), and pp.130-131.

Sándor and Gizella Ferenczi to Georg and Emmy Groddeck

Capri, 17th October 1931

Dear Pat and Emke,

Until a few days ago it still looked like it does on this card,[1] and now we've been shivering for 3 days in an unheated Hotel Quisisana. Raging winds and rain non-stop. I'm sorry to hear from Mrs Kovács that you, dear Pat, have been unwell.[2] I hope that you are already much better. We're back in Budapest on the 1st.

Your Sándor.

I was very sorry to hear that you, Pat, have been ill – all I can do is wish you a speedy recovery and hope that you can soon set off

99

on your trip in the best of health and spirits. We are already on our homeward journey in our thoughts and are looking forward to a well-heated home. Embracing you both in loving friendship

Your

Gizella

[1] Postcard showing a photo of Sándor and Gizella on donkeys in the sunshine of Capri.
[2] What illness Groddeck had is not clear: it may have been a stroke, but was called a heart attack (*The Wild Analyst*, p.180).

Sándor Ferenczi to Georg Groddeck

GRAND HOTEL QUISISANA, CAPRI

Capri, 21st October 1931

Dear Pat,

I have just heard via Sarolta that you cannot make up your minds about where to spend your winter holiday.

In my opinion, there are only two places worth considering: Palermo or Algiers. Climatically speaking, the latter is perhaps best, but the crossing by sea can be rather long during bad weather. Palermo is undoubtedly very lovely, except for the occasional sirocco days. There are (just as in Algiers) good hotels with bathrooms. The deep hinterland behind Palermo offers a variety of excursions; you can get everywhere by automobile. Villa Igila is very expensive. When I was in Palermo[1] with Prof. Freud we stayed in the Hotel de France, which had a bath that worked well. We were very satisfied. It cost about half as much as the Hotel-Villa Igila.

Capri is out of the question. The island is beautiful, but you've seen it all in next to no time, and the weather is unreliable. We have shivered here for days on end with no central heating. On nice days, though, it is incomparably beautiful here.

It makes me happy to think of you perhaps ambling through the gardens of Palermo whilst we, in the rest of Europe, freeze. I'm convinced it's the one ideal place for you.

Taormina[2] is, I hear, very beautiful, but not as animating as Palermo – and much too small for a longer stay. But for complete peace the place may be suitable. I have never been there.

I would like to hear soon what you have decided on. In the meantime, greetings from your

Sándor

We will be home on 31st October. (Lisznyai u.11, Budapest).

[1] For Ferenczi's time with Freud in Palermo, see pp.8-9, Christmas 1921 letter.
[2] Small town on the east coast of Sicily, below Messina.

Sándor and Gizella Ferenczi to Georg and Emmy Groddeck[1]

Piazza San Marco, 26th October 1931

Here we are sitting in the Café Florian, just as we did with you. We can't pass by Venice without stopping off here. Of course we think of you all the time, and wish you a happy holiday.

Sándor

101

We're waiting for news from you – how you are – and where you're off to on your winter trip. Please write to Budapest very soon.

Gizella.

[1] Postcard with picture of Piazza San Marco, Venice, Italy, on reverse.

Sándor Ferenczi to Georg Groddeck

DR. S. FERENCZI

BUDAPEST I. LISZNYAI U. 11

3rd November 1931

Dear Pat,

Just a few lines about your winter plans. We hear wonders about the pleasant, warm and envigorating winter climate of Merano,[1] (now Italy), where natural beauty combines with *haute cuisine* and a high standard of accommodation; with bathrooms and central heating everywhere. Someone told us that even the last weeks of October – when storms raged throughout the rest of Europe – were mild and pleasant in Merano.

We are so pleased to hear that you are feeling better.[2]

I started work again today.

Greetings to you both from us all,

Your Sándor

[1] Merano, a town in the Trentino – Alto Adige, just south of the Austrian border and north of Bolzano in northern Italy.
[2] See n.2, p.100, regarding Groddeck's illness.

Sándor Ferenczi to Georg and Emmy Groddeck[1]

DR. S. FERENCZI
BUDAPEST I. LISZNYAI U. 11

3rd March 1932

Dear Friends,

Thank you for your detailed reports, which, thank God, sound positive this time. I don't know what to admire more: Emke's or Pat's unshakeable spirit of optimism, which triumphs over all indications of illness.

As to myself, I cannot tell you in a word how I'm feeling. Relatively well physically speaking, I alternate mentally between great activity and extreme fatigue. Matters which occupy me intellectually have still not matured to the point where I could communicate them. My 'scientific imagination', although 'well-disciplined' (Freud), induces me to fly beyond the unconscious at times to the so-called metaphysical, which I find reflected in almost identical form in the material my patients produce. There seems to be a path which leads from dreams to a deeper under-standing of the splitting of the personality, and psychoses too. I owe my technical advances to what my patients tell me about their own resistances.[2]

The latest innovation here is that a psychoanalytic out-patient clinic[3] has been set up, with which the Kovács family is very involved. The Congress has been postponed till the end of August, but won't – I feel – take place then either.[4]

Quite honestly, I sometimes envy you, dear Pat, that you're

ill;[5] it must be very pleasant recuperating in your house and in the garden. I hope that these few lines will suffice to remind you of us. We do hope to get good news soon.

Financially things aren't looking too rosy for me either, as I'm only earning about half as much as in previous years. But in view of the overall depression, things aren't so bad.

All the best, and love from us both,

Your Sándor

[1] Ferenczi addressed this typed letter with letterhead to Groddeck at Hans Thoma Strasse 8, Baden-Baden, but it was redirected to Groddeck: c/o Mrs. van Ergehen Boissevain, Naarden, Muntweg 5, Holland.

[2] Ferenczi is alluding to a very intense period of work. As already mentioned, it was in 1932 – from January until October – that he wrote his *Clinical Diary* (1932), which conveys in great detail personal disclosures about his work and himself, his ideas, and his clinical explorations. One of the 'technical advances' he was involved with at the time was a mutual analysis with his patient and pupil, Elizabeth Severn. His reference to the metaphysical certainly would, to some degree at least, refer to the domain both Severn and Ferenczi felt they were exploring (for example, Severn felt she could do 'telepathic healing' (Ferenczi, 1932, p.158). On 1st May 1932, Ferenczi writes to Freud that he is 'immersing [himself] in a kind of scientific "poetry and truth".' While much of his work remained in the diary, Ferenczi does share some of his thinking at this time in his final paper, 'Confusion of tongues between adults and the child' (1933).

[3] At 12 Meszaros Street, at the bottom of Lisznyai Street, on which the Ferenczis lived. See also n.3, p.95.

[4] An International Psycho-Analytical Congress was to be held in September 1931 at Interlaken, Switzerland. However, a number of factors – the world economic crisis, the grave political situation with the rise of national socialism in Germany, the collapse of the Vienna Kreditanstalt Bank – led to it being cancelled. In 1932, the Congress was relocated to Wiesbaden, Germany, because the Germans couldn't obtain funds to travel outside their country. As it turned out, Ferenczi was overly pessimistic as the Congress was, in fact, held 4th-7th September 1932. Ominously, the Congress was held under the surveillance of German police.

[5] This theme of Ferenczi's fatigue has been evident in his letters for the last few years.

Sándor Ferenczi to Georg and Emmy Groddeck

DR. S. FERENCZI   BUDAPEST I. LISZNYAI U. 11
                                                            20th March 1933

Dear Friends!

It seems that one cannot sin and go unpunished, least of all for years on end.[1] My indisposition in Baden-Baden[2] was the beginning of an extremely dangerous anaemia which almost struck me down in France, so that I only just managed to drag myself home – prematurely.[3] Since then I'm working at half steam and am being fed subcutaneously with liver. My condition is, apart from the occasional fluctuation, relatively satisfactory now. The underlying psychological reason for this decline was due, apart from sheer exhaustion, to my disappointment in Freud,[4] about which you also know. We have stopped corresponding for the time being, although both of us are trying to salvage what can be salvaged. I'm sure that, in the end, we will more or less succeed in doing so.[5] I am, as always, full of ideas, though the desire to pen them equals zero. A short, complete break should get my strength up, though where to go in these depressing times?[6]

I admire your stamina and your enthusiasm not to have given up, despite illness and difficulties. Your new book,[7] whose contents were quite familiar to me, is arousing much interest among all those to whom I have given it to read. I am beginning to think that your strength of mind will surmount all difficulties. N.B. Her ladyship, the Countess, is no longer with me.[8]

My wife is well and assists me unfailingly. Sarolta is here at present; she is due for her operations on both cataracts this

105

week and next. She's exceptionally brave. Elma is doing well as a civil servant in the American Consulate. Magda is all right[9] since her appendix operation.

In adding that this is the first letter in a long time to put me in touch with the outside world, which is no doubt a sign of our indestructible friendship, I remain, with thanks for your news,

Your old Sándor

[1] The tone of this sentence reminds one of the last lines of Ferenczi's (1932) *Clinical Diary* (p.215): 'Catalogue of Sins... There must be punishment. (Contrition.)'

[2] The Ferenczis went to the sanatorium for a short stay after the Wiesbaden Congress.

[3] After Baden-Baden the Ferenczis went to Biarritz in the south-west of France.

[4] Ferenczi's relations with Freud were strained during the last years. This situation came to a head in late August 1932 when Ferenczi, on his way to the Wiesbaden Congress (4-7 September), visited Freud in Vienna to read him his 'Confusion of tongues', the paper he would present at the Congress. The charged meeting – Freud told Ferenczi he should not publish the paper – ended with Freud refusing to shake Ferenczi's outstretched hand (Jones, 1957, also confirmed by Thompson, de Forest and Fromm; see also *The Freud-Ferenczi Correspondence*, Vol. III, pp.442-3). Sadly, this was to be the last meeting of these two long-time friends, and the encounter left Ferenczi feeling discouraged and depressed.

[5] Ferenczi and Freud resumed some correspondence over the next months. It seems that they never did make a complete break, and, in fact, in the letters they made a mutual attempt to put their differences aside, since they were both dealing with other important issues, including their health.

[6] A reference to the rise of Fascism in Europe – specifically the Nazis in Germany. On 10th May 1933 in Berlin the Nazi book burnings took place, which included both Ferenczi's and Groddeck's works. Ferenczi felt very apprehensive and, in fact, warned Freud in his letter of 29th March 1933 to leave Vienna for his own safety.

[7] *Der Mensch als Symbol: Unmassgebliche Meinungen über Sprache und Kunst* [Man as Symbol: Unauthoritative Views on Language and Art], Leipzig/Vienna: Internationaler Psychoanalytischer Verlag, 1933. Partially reprinted in *Psychoanalytische Schriften zur Literatur und Kunst*. Reissued by Limes Verlag, Wiesbaden, 1973, (no English translation). The book was sent to Freud who confirmed to Groddeck the permanence of his esteem. This book was to have been completed by a second person who was to have analysed humankind according to the body's different organs.

[8] 'the Countess' refers to Elizabeth Severn, who ended her work with Ferenczi in late February, 1933 (Fortune, 1993, 1994).

[9] 'all right' in English in the original.

This typed letter was the last letter Ferenczi wrote to Groddeck.
Ferenczi died 22nd May 1933, at 2:30pm.

106

Gizella Ferenczi to Georg and Emmy Groddeck

14th July 1933[1]

My dear Friends,

In my sorrow I turn to you again today, my dearest ones – because I am so immeasurably sad. I cannot adjust at all to the thought of living without Sándor – I need him from morning to night – every thought belongs only to him – and everything is so unimportant, so meaningless if I cannot share it with him, if he isn't listening or looking. All I want to do is to cry all day long, but I can't because of the others. So many old people go on living, so many of them are sick. Why did it have to be Sándor who had to leave this world he loved so very much. It is incomprehensible. I thought to visit you in July for a few days, but I have to consider Magda and her husband who cannot get away before August. It will be very difficult for me to travel to B.B. – to you, where Sándor and I spent so many happy days – I don't know whether I can manage it at all the way I am feeling at present. Everything still hurts too much.

A few days ago I heard from Erdös Pista[2] that you are in Switzerland. Is one of you ill? Or were you invited? You must write to me, my dearest friends, because this news worries me. Forgive me if I break off now, I can't go on.

As ever in love and friendship, I remain your

Gizella

---

[1] Written exactly one week after what would have been Sándor's 60th birthday – 7th July 1933. The letter has a bold black border conveying the mourning period for Ferenczi's death. No location is given.
[2] Zsofia Ferenczi's husband.

Gizella Ferenczi to Georg and Emmy Groddeck

2nd November 1933

My dear dear Friends!

What shall I say – what shall I write? I just don't know. You can imagine the state I'm in. I cannot come to terms with the fact that Sándor is no more, that I will never see him again, never look after him again – that he has left life, this earth of which he was so very much a part. He didn't ever want to die, for he loved life. Do you remember, Pat, how often he would say, 'This is where I would like to die, here with you', and all the time he was so ill I often wished I could be with you. I have told you how ill Sándor became on his autumn trip, but he recovered quickly, once he was home, and spent the four winter months working without any anxieties. By March, however, Sándor was already so weak that he had to stop giving sessions – and we thought a long break until September would help get him over his frailty. Unfortunately, the illness he had – pernicious anaemia – knows no mercy, and he just got weaker and weaker. He had to be put to bed because his feet wouldn't carry him any more – his mind began to give[1] and he spent four weeks in bed. On the twenty-second of May, the day he died, he was still speaking to us, read the newspaper (which kept on dropping out of his hands) and called for Sarolta to tell her: 'Sarolta, "revisions" will be necessary.'[2] Then we saw that he quite suddenly became very weak. The three of us wanted some black coffee, though Sándor wanted his cold, and by the time we got back to his bed we saw that the end was imminent. Since that moment I cannot pull myself together and don't know how to go on living with my great yearning for him. I thank you for your sweet, kind words and thank you for loving Sándor – I know that you are with me in my sorrow and feel for me. We intended to visit you in the summer, only Sándor thought that the situation[3] there wouldn't permit it. It is possible that I may see you in the summer because I have to make a small trip. With a heavy heart and great sadness I embrace you.

Your Gizella

P.S. Dear Friends, I cannot thank fate enough that I had my double eye operation before Sándor became so ill, and could therefore spend so much time at his bedside. He was so sweet, forgiving, loving and patient throughout his illness. He spoke with great affection of you before he died, and was aware of your love for him, which made him very happy.

Desperately sad,

Your Sarolta.

Elma and Magda, and all friends, are with Gizella in her loss, and are rallying round her.

---

[1] This line was excised from the version published in *The Wild Analyst*, (p.191).

[2] Balint (1949), who was near Ferenczi during the weeks before his death, wrote that Ferenczi had intended to modify or 'revise' the controversial views he put forward in 'Confusion of tongues'.

[3] Hitler's rise to power and anti-Semitism.

Gizella Ferenczi to Georg and Emmy Groddeck[1]

9th January 1934

My dear Friends,

Your letters written with friendship and love are among the few joys I experienced this Christmas. It did my heart good to be able to count you amongst my friends, to know that our thoughts and feelings are united in harmony. It would have hurt Sándor and me if it had been otherwise. I cannot agree with you on one matter, though, dear Emke, namely that Sándor intuitively chose to die, for he loved life, wanted to enjoy it, to embrace everything, be it good or bad – beautiful or ugly – and live – live in this world. It becomes more and more incomprehensible with every passing day: why this death? I cannot adjust to it. Since May 22nd it feels like a continuous farewell to everything – and lonely. Only when my thoughts turn to my children do I feel a link to life.

Frau Lou Salomé writes to me very sweetly at times. Amongst other things, she asks: "Couldn't Groddeck, who knew Sándor's body so <u>completely</u>, have advised and done something? You are still 'in touch' with the Groddecks, no doubt?" Further: "I think so often about what happened and how Ferenczi himself would have thought about it, as life and death meant something quite different to him from what it does to other people. His manner and wonderful temperament banished any intimation of death, even urged life out of death itself." I have copied this because it shows how incomprehensible it all is for her too.

I never hear anything from the Freuds. My letters and New

Year's greetings remain unanswered – why? – I don't know. Perhaps I unintentionally did something wrong, or does the family no longer want anything to do with us, with Sándor and me? However that may be, my great admiration, loyalty and love for the Professsor will die only when I do.[2]

I hear that Jones, in London, wrote an article in the 'Journal'[3] against Sándor, particularly against his genital theory. Perhaps Miss Collins[4] – to whom I send my fondest greetings – may know something about it. 'Baroness' Severn has apparently also published a book – which won't please the orthodox Freudians.[5]

I would have liked to have read your London lectures, dear Pat, but how and where can I get hold of them? I am so very sorry to hear that you are suffering; please get well and stay well for all our sakes. And dear Emke writes nothing about you, though reading between the lines I can feel that you are in good spirits, and take life as it is. How wise!!

I read everything you write with interest, my dearest friend, and cannot get enough of it. I am glad that Britta[6] is happy in her job and that she can spend the whole holiday with you. How lovely it must be just now, right in the middle of the wood.[7]

Sarolta, Elma and I live *au trois* now – only Sándor isn't here, who made everything come alive with his magnificent personality. – Sarolta has been suffering for weeks from boils. She takes hip baths and heat treatment, and is on a diet, so things are slowly on the mend.

Elma is going to America in April to see her friends – and Elsie – but mainly to have a three month holiday which she badly needs. She wants me to come, but it's too expensive for me at the moment. The Morandos[8] aren't well off either.

Thank you, dear Emke, for your invitation. The journey to Switzerland, which was not necessary last year, will probably have to take place this year – I will definitely come then. How I miss you both!

With an affectionate embrace from your faithful Gizella

[1] Black border around edges of letter. No location written.
[2] We must remember the long-standing connection Gizella herself had with Freud: he had enthusiastically encouraged Ferenczi to marry her; and Freud had special feelings for Gizella which are reflected by personal greetings in letters to Ferenczi, and in his own letters to Gizella.
[3] *The International Journal of Psycho-Analysis.*
[4] See n.10, p.74.
[5] In the autumn of 1933, Elizabeth Severn published *The Discovery of the Self.* (London: Rider). Ferenczi describes his initial antipathy to her as partly due to her 'somewhat sovereign, majestic superiority of a queen, or even the royal imperiousness of a king... characteristics that one certainly cannot call feminine' (*Clinical Diary*, p.97).
[6] Britta, Emmy Groddeck's niece.
[7] In Groddeck's hut in the woods.
[8] That is, Gizella's sister Sarolta, and her husband Otto Morando.

Georg Groddeck to Gizella Ferenczi

19th February 1934

Dear Gizella,

I have for a long time wondered whether I should write this letter or not, but I have now decided to do so. I'm typing this because it is the only way I can express myself with sufficient objectivity.

All these last years I could only think about Sándor's life with a heavy heart. He became the victim of his own spirit of inquiry, a fate I escaped only because of my insufficient thirst for know-ledge.[1] I must first speak about myself. Even before going over to psychoanalysis one of the underlying principles of my medical thinking was the conviction that in human individuals there are – apart from the psyche which is the subject of scientific inves-tigation – thousands and millions of more or less independently existing souls which continuously unite and separate, group and re-group, working sometimes for and sometimes against each other, and probably exist quite independently at times. Having embraced this view, I was content to leave it at that. I never tried to study this cosmos; it simply isn't in my nature to go into matters which I consider unfathomable.[2]

Being such a close friend of Sándor's, I soon realised that he viewed these matters similarly. I was thus horrified to see him proceed to investigate this human cosmos scientifically, even attempt to describe it, so that others could participate in this undoubtedly overwhelming spectacle. He became completely consumed by this endeavour. He expressed it thus to me: I atomise the soul. Such atomisation, though, if pursued seriously, can only end in the dissolution of the self, for another human being is, and always will remain hidden to us. We can only atomise our own soul, and that will destroy us. The manner in which Sándor, whose genius and courage I always admired, was finally released from this superhuman effort is immaterial. I did at times try to point out the dangers of this path. But you could no more stem a roaring current with a cupped hand than help Sándor. If some should say that I, perhaps, could have helped him, they are wrong. However close we may have been, and however great our friendship, he had already left me far behind in his ascent to the stars, which I couldn't and wouldn't join. This is all I can tell you. External events only acquired meaning in the life of this rare human being as he belonged to the givers, to those who give again and again.[3]

[1] Groddeck encapsulates the basic difference between himself and Sándor – a difference they had noted time and again in their letters.

[2] This paragraph summarises aspects of Groddeck's philosophy – one in which he feels we are lived by the 'It.'

[3] The only existing typed copy of this letter, without location, ends here. Groddeck's analysis of his friend Sándor is an insightful addition to other obituaries of Ferenczi by Freud, et al., including Freud's description of Ferenczi in 'Analysis terminable and interminable' (1937).

Gizella Ferenczi to Georg Groddeck

28th February 1934[1]

Your letter – dear Pat – upset and profoundly disturbed me. I can see that you too needed time to reflect before you could answer me, in order to make your position clear. It was probably unconsidered of me to quote Lou Salomé's words to you. I never thought that you could have read anything else into them than the greatest confidence in your abilities – a view I share with her. I was so happy that she was so appreciative and believes in you so strongly that I made haste to repeat her words to you.

The experiences of the last years showed me that nobody – not even you – could help him.[2] A gradual transformation in him not only began to destroy his body, but also had an enormous influence on his mental life. His 'ascent to the stars', as you put it so beautifully, took him such immense distances that he himself lost sight of the final goal. This desperate brooding, his struggle with knowledge and conscience, his constant questioning of the results of his research – all this served to undermine his health in mind and body and brought about his decline. His diseased and eventually wholly-destroyed kidney was also a contributory factor, don't you think? If there was anyone who did him good in his battle whilst he was still master of himself, it was you. You yourself know how rejuvenated he always was when he left you, how he loved being with you – and nobody had such a continuous influence on him as you – my dear Pat. Don't ever for a moment think that I intended to blame you. In my heart I have nothing but love and gratitude for you. Not only that you always attended to Sándor as his physician, but that you, as no other, loved, appreciated and honoured him. The days we spent in your midst were happy, harmonious and successful ones for both of us. It's almost a year since Sándor left us – to me it seems like yesterday.

I embrace my Emke, and hope to visit you this year. We can talk things over then.

Affectionately,

Gizella

---

[1] There is still a black border of mourning around letter, nine months after Ferenczi's death. No salutation.

[2] Freud passed on Gizella's view of Ferenczi to Jones: 'His [Ferenczi's] perceptive and good wife conveyed to me that I should think of him as a sick child' (Freud to Jones, 12th September 1932, *Freud-Jones Correspondence*).

Extracts from Letters of Frédéric Kovács

to

Vilma Kovács

7th January–27th February 1927

As an appendix to this correspondence between Ferenczi and Groddeck, we offer some extracts from a series of letters written by
Frédéric Kovács, who was taking a cure at Baden-Baden in Dr Groddeck's sanatorium, to his wife Vilma Kovács, who had remained in
Budapest. The letters were written in Hungarian.

In his letters to Groddeck, Ferenczi mentions the Kovács couple
on several occasions. After she had been his patient, Vilma Kovács
became Ferenczi's student, and then one of the important members
of the Budapest Psychoanalytic Association, particularly interested,
among other things, in the problems of training analysts. A divorced
woman with three children – a rarity at this time – she had married
Kovács, an architect, who adopted and raised the three children.

The older daughter, Alice, was Michael Balint's wife. She died in
Manchester in August 1939. A psychoanalyst herself, she published
many articles, and a little book translated into many languages,
particularly French: *Psychoanalysis of the Nursery* (Routledge &
Kegan Paul, London 1953). The younger daughter, Olga, was an
artist. Together with Robert Berény, she drew the series of caricatures at the International Congress of Psychoanalysis at Salzburg in
1924, the one which is mentioned in a note accompanying the
Ferenczi-Groddeck correspondence (see p.52, note 5). François, the
youngest child, became an architect like his step-father.

Vilma and Frédéric Kovács were personal friends of the Ferenczis.
This is how Ferenczi was led to refer Frédéric Kovács – a tall, large
man suffering from various cardiac, circulatory and digestive troubles
of uncertain origin – to Groddeck; after hesitating for a long time,
Frédéric Kovács finally decided to take a cure at the beginning of
1927, a cure followed by some more. This first cure lasted seven
weeks, from 7th January until 28th February 1927, during which he
wrote his wife a letter every day. In these letters he recorded, day
after day, not to say hour after hour, all the details of his life in
the sanatorium, and of his treatment, as well as all the conversations that he had with Groddeck. The letters of this affectionate
husband, who used every spare minute to note something for his
wife, allow us to become acquainted with the atmosphere which
reigned inside the 'Satanarium', which was recalled so often with
nostalgia by Ferenczi, and with the way in which the people taking
the cure lived, were treated and enjoyed themselves. They also give
us an insight into the type of transference which was established
between Dr Groddeck and his patients.

7th January 1927

My little darling,

....

I arrived here on the dot of half past seven in the evening, a manservant came to fetch me and, contrary to my expectation – I thought that it would be a little seedy sanatorium with minuscule rooms in a narrow street – the car brought me to an area of villas, in front of a building in the middle of a beautiful garden, where I was allocated a very pleasant, spacious and light room. This is what it is like [there follows a plan]. To the front, a charming oriel window, entirely glazed, with a view onto the town, the room, like the oriel, delightfully arranged; my bed is excellent and everything is of an extraordinary, exemplary cleanliness. The cooking is excellent and sophisticated. Groddeck came to visit me the same evening, for a brief moment, and this morning he carried out a pounding on me which would have done justice to a 200-kilo Cossack. You can imagine that after that, the forty respiratory movements were nothing but a light breath. Then he promised me that for 4-5 days he would give me little to eat and even less to drink (this last point scarcely worries me, because he has allowed me black coffee). I can also smoke my cigar, which I am very glad about because it makes the time pass more easily. – For the same period, he has prescribed hot baths, each day for a different part of the body; today, for example, I had an arm bath (37° R[éaumur]), but I sweated everywhere, completely, like a horse. He has told me not to go walking for the time being. This is all the more easy to tolerate because I wouldn't have been able to anyway, and also because it is pouring with rain. Otherwise, you know me, I am always in a hurry to see the place where I am.

I have already protested against a crazy custom. Breakfast is brought to you here at half past seven in the morning, although the sun doesn't begin to rise until a quarter to nine. I have said that when it is dark, I want to sleep. In any case, I don't know what to do all day long. Now it is midday, all these events which I have told you have happened during the day; ah yes, he also said to me, Groddeck, that this stomach of mine, it was truly appalling. Of course, medicines are forbidden, but he allowed me to take the pills if I felt ill. Now, immediately, as soon as I have finished this letter, I shall go and take a walk in front of the house; I want to

119

sniff the air here, in broad daylight. At 1.30 it will be a famine lunch, I shall not even have any fruit, and in the afternoon I shall read and do God knows what. At 8 o'clock, Groddeck comes back to see me. He only has three patients apart from me, so he has time to devote to me.

....

That's all I can write for today, except that I love you very much, my darling.

Fri.[1]

8th January 1927

Imagine, my little darling, what Groddeck told me yesterday when he made his regular visit to me: Ferenczi loved Gizella first, then he got engaged to Elma; but the engagement was broken off, and she got married in America, and it was then that Ferenczi married Gizella. What do you say to that? What's more, Gizella's dearest wish, at present, and her plan, is that Sándor should divorce her and marry Elma – she would not give him up for any other woman, only for Elma – and she would content herself with playing the role of mother. After all, Gizella is in her 62nd year and Elma is only just over 40; that's why Elma went from Paris to Berlin, to see Groddeck – who was there for a round of lectures – because she was very depressed. According to Frau Groddeck, Elma 'war nahe am Erlöschen',[2] so great were – that is to say, are – her conflicts; Groddeck got her back on her feet to a certain extent, and Elma decided either to move to Berlin, or perhaps to take a separate flat in Budapest, but not to stay any more in the shared flat.

So this is what was so apparent in this poor, pitiable, marvellous creature. One should really look after her a bit – insofar as she allows it – she must be very unhappy.

I started to write this letter at 11.30, after finishing my toilette. Earlier, there was a new kneading and massage, and then I had to do 40 squats in a row – let's pass over those – for all this time, my only pleasure was in thinking that I would be rid of this form of entertainment until the evening. For then Groddeck will come to trample out of me what he himself laughingly calls dinner. This morning I have already had a sitz bath which, on the one hand, boiled me scarlet like a redskin, and on the other hand made me sweat like

120

a piece of heavy artillery firing rain. My so-called food consists of the following: in the morning, coffee, roll with a bit of butter on it. During the morning, soft white cheese or an egg, with 15 gr. of bread. Dinner: 80 gr. of meat with 15 gr. of bread and black coffee. Needless to say, I am so starving that the next time I think I shall eat the decorative parsley, or whatever else there is. In the afternoon, tea (which I don't drink) and a buttered roll, and in the evening a bit of fish with lots of bones, probably to make it last longer – always trimmed with some green herb; 15 gr. of bread and black coffee – no vegetables, no fruit, no drink of any sort, not even water, so that after the coffee I quickly light a cigar to forget even the simple fact that one has to eat. By the way, they are absolutely delighted, because in a day and a half they have relieved me of 1.5 kilos.

The sun has just come out, until now it was raining all the time, and Frau Groddeck is getting ready to leave with two friends who are visiting here – just as Swedish as her; bags on their backs, they are going into the mountains to spend their Sunday there; it was still raining when they left, I seriously wonder what they are going to do there. She told me that I had to go too one day! Groddeck himself will go there tomorrow; he has his Sunday on Mondays. I was very sad that everyone was going and that the house was emptying, although that changes nothing, I never see anyone during the day. Frau Groddeck told me to come up and see them in the evening, and to take advantage of the company of their guests, but as for them, they drink, which could be difficult for me. – Until now I have gone nowhere; it seems that he wants first to plane me down; for the moment, he doesn't allow me to walk; he doesn't do anything else to me, he hasn't really even questioned me properly. But apparently he knows everything: what happened last year and everything which is in my letter, because from time to time he puts a question, here and there, which demonstrates his information, or his good memory. It seems that I am not missing work much, and I feel fine doing nothing and reading. The music from the Casino drifts up here, and brings a bit of animation into my marvellous room, and then there are a few roosters, also very intelligent, because they don't start to crow until 9.30. Goodbye, my darling, lead a pleasant and joyful life. I kiss you a million times.

Fri.

9th January 1927

....

...What I feared most – boredom – has not yet appeared. And yet, how lonely I am! You cannot even imagine it. I see the chambermaid, who brings my crumbs, and you can imagine how much I adore her; the manservant who looks after the heating; and the bath lady who scalds me disagreeably. In the afternoon the *Hausdame*[3] (an old maid) comes to find out how I am – and then the doctor who utters practically not a word, but contents himself with poking, measuring and weighing. However, the result, at least until now, is excellent, a further kilo lost during the second day; and yesterday, although walking is not recommended for me at the moment, I forgot everything and went walking for 25 minutes in the mountains ... The villas – amongst which Groddeck's stands – are built along the roads which snake as they climb, and very near the town, of which I know nothing up to now – although it is already Sunday – I have not yet moved from here and therefore I have no idea what is hiding behind that marvellous panorama which I enjoy from my window. There, in front of me, lies the town, and behind, in a semi-circle, rises a large mountain up which a funicular leads ... and at the summit, a panoramic viewpoint.

....

In the meantime, Uncle Groddeck comes to my room to trample my guts out of my body, so that he can enjoy his weekend in peace. I shall not see him again today, nor tomorrow. He was very pleased with me ... But things would only really be good if you were here with me ... I asked Groddeck today about this, but sadly he said that later, perhaps, he would see no reason why not, if I felt too lonely, but that it was better if family members were not here.

... She (Frau Groddeck) does not dare tackle my gigantic tummy. But on the other hand, she is all the more attentively vigilant – as she told me – about cleanliness; everything is veritably shining, and the food is also impeccable and very correctly served. Yesterday, for dinner, I had two eggs, but from now on without any garnish, it seems that they have noticed that I have difficulty in resisting greenery. I also had 15 gr. of bread for dinner, some coffee, then quickly, my cigar.

....

10th January 1927

....

Otherwise, my day has passed well. In the morning, Groddeck came to plunge his antennae vigorously into me, and he certainly made me sweat with his impressive weight. – Then, without any pain, either during, or after, I took a normal bath. In the afternoon, for the first time, I ventured to explore the town. I went to the Casino – the descent went reasonably well; I found nothing interesting there, apart from a pretty reading room; I missed the concert, I shall perhaps get there more punctually today, if my numerous commitments leave me time to do so ...

13th January 1927

....

If things go on like this, what will be left of me? My little darling, today I have lost another kilo, with the result that in 5 days of cure, that man Groddeck has taken 6 kilos from me.

...

Tap, tap! – I hear an unfamiliar knocking; what on earth is going on? – Here comes Frau Groddeck hurtling into my room; it is a patient's birthday, do I want to take part, everyone will be there, and I will have dispensation for today, I will be allowed to eat and drink as much as I want. The following instant, a new irruption; she enters laden with a heap of clothes, disguises me as a noble oriental, concocts me a turban, scarves, a kaftan and heaven knows what else, and now here I am, turban on my head, I no longer have the right to take it off and I am waiting for what happens next. It will start an hour from now, at 8.30; the whole of this floor is decorated with paper lanterns, and now I must put on some make-up. So everything has changed from one minute to the next. – I will continue writing tomorrow morning, because I must prepare myself, and then it will be time for dinner. – Half an hour has passed, it seems that they have deliberately forgotten about the usual dinner and I'm dying of thirst, I've drunk nothing during the day, not even tea, so that I will have the right to drink a spritzer[4] this evening. Too bad, I'll make up for it ...

Well, we've had the ball. We were received in a room plunged into half-light; Uncle Groddeck was Nero, with the help of two sheets and a crown of leaves; as for me, doubtless thanks to the excellence of my make-up, he didn't recognise me. We spent the night sitting on cushions on the floor, and periodically we were brought food and drink. I don't know who was there, one could scarcely see – there were most of the people in the house; among them, an analyst from Berlin, Liebermann,[5] who knows you. I even danced, I executed the Hungarian national dance[6] to the music of a foxtrot. At a quarter to four, we were sent to bed. Meanwhile, Groddeck had already left on two separate occasions ...

14th January 1927

....

The women who are on duty at night, I've only seen one of them, but I'm not even sure whether it might have been the chamber-maid ... you know, all these Swedish beanpoles look alike. This one is, I believe, Frau Groddeck's niece; the Doctor's daughter[7] was there too ... not saying a word ... Groddeck congratulated me for having substantially contributed to the success of the party ... But it is true that it was really good, and I felt I should do my duty towards my country: I had to show them what it is to have some temperament.

....

It is true that I put on nearly a kilo that night, but I said to Groddeck that it wasn't surprising, I had downed a good litre of champagne – yet he maintained that I was making a mistake and that I had downed a great deal more; however, he reckons that it isn't serious, that what one puts on in that way falls off again easily, and in any case, it is good from time to time to rinse out the body.

... This Liebermann was very ill when he arrived here around Christmas; he was totally overworked – he says that he was working 98 hours per week. Now he is as happy as a lark; he fooled about a lot last night. One of the women was also very funny ... suddenly she jumped on me from behind when I was on my knees in front of another woman, in the process of tearing off her newspaper-dress ... Towards two o'clock I suddenly thought that I might be sick, and I nearly took a pill, but I didn't let myself go and, afterwards, the madcap behaviour continued unabated until Frau Groddeck sent us to bed. If she hadn't, we would still be there. They have a delightful flat, but I'll tell you about that another time.

....

15th January 1927

....

For some days, I haven't stopped thinking how marvellous it would be to come back with Olga.[8] After hesitating a long time, I none the less dared to raise the question; on this, Uncle Sphinx replied quite calmly: 'Ja, was weiss ich, das müssen Sie besser wissen.'[9] At this a discussion ensued, that it was out of the question, that it was he who was the expert – you know how it goes: he is not a prophet, everything depends on me, then a charming smile, I am your humble servant – and with that he left me standing there. However, we chatted for a long time today because this morning – for the first time since I have been here – I didn't feel quite well; I didn't have any pains, but I was very annoyed about what all this might mean; in fact, I burped a great deal, and that was all. Of course, I went immediately to complain about it. Instead of giving me pills, he asked me what I had against the cure, because in his opinion that was where we should look for the problem, that is to say, the cause; I said: nothing; he said: perhaps it's too expensive; ah, I said: I've already accepted it. And so on. I got things off my chest and then everything was fine; to the point that at the end of the 40th trampling I had only counted 30, so little had I felt them.

... I wonder why I'm giving you all these details; everything will get better, I trust Groddeck; I might add that he asked me about that very question today and told me that if he couldn't be sure of this and if I were to stop trusting, he would not be able to cure me. So there we are, now it's over to me to keep an eye on trust, because if I mislay it, I'll have no choice but to take a running jump.

... At the ball, it seemed that Nero somewhat loosened his tongue and relaxed his discretion: he told me, *à propos* of Elma, that in the family circle in which she found herself she would not be able to recover; he was very happy when I told him that she was going to move.

... I'm not even hungry, I have got quite used to not eating. But yesterday, I was furious; they made me swallow a piece of boiled meat without sauté potatoes, mustard, sauce, anything, just a tiny piece of bread. That was lunch. For all my money!

16 January 1927

....

In the evening, I became alarmed at the idea of what would happen if I was ill in the night. There are no staff on this floor ... Groddeck reassured me today, saying that the bell is connected to him during the night and that, if I wanted, he would have a push-button installed by my bed – I told him that I didn't need it ...

....

This evening, Liebermann came to visit me; he is very nice to me. Tomorrow he is taking me on a walk and to the theatre. Groddeck is naturally in the know about everything, and he approves. This evening, too, Groddeck was very encouraging with me – however, it is true that, even 'when one looks after a broken leg, one can never foresee everything which might happen.'

....

17th January 1927

My little darling, today everything was upside down. The bath lady was apparently not satisfied with my loss of half a kilo, so she made me sweat terribly in the hip bath; when she finally let me out, Groddeck was already with someone else and I had to wait for his visit until midday ... By the way, we had an important conversation, I told him about my tax problems – which, clearly, are preoccupying me a great deal – and afterwards it was better. Today, while walking, I began to feel how much lighter I have become; I have less weight to carry ... After lunch, Liebermann took me to a marvellous thermal and steam bath ... An indescribable order rules there, and it is full of paunchy gentlemen, fatter than me: it was worth the trouble of going just for that. Arrows indicate the order in which you are supposed to go from the different rooms at 60° and 70° of steam and into the pools; when you come out, they put hot slippers of an immaculate whiteness on your feet, and also a cap and dressing-gown, and they transfer you onto a chaise longue and wrap you up so that you can rest. Meanwhile, a masseur tries to get hold of you, but I jumped out of the way, because Groddeck is enough for me...

18th January 1927

....

There is a captain of the Hussars here from what was once our country,[10] now a medical student in Berlin, who has married Melanie Klein's daughter – he is called Schmideberg, and it seems that he is very ill. I have not yet met him, because at the moment he is in Berlin for a few days, for his wife's birthday ...

For the moment, I am no longer losing weight ... But Groddeck explains to me persistently and very learnedly that this is perfectly normal and that in any case this isn't what is important, but rather that he listens while he auscultates my muscles. So I said that although he claims that I always persist in my stubborn judgement because I'm like that, I am sincerely convinced that he knows about these things better than I do, and that's why I've come to him.

...

24th January 1927

... I have had rather a bad day ... Yesterday, during treatment, I had an attack. But much less intense than at home, and that angel Groddeck behaved as if he didn't care; and when he went, I was free of it. Yesterday he came three times, because the first time passed so quickly that he didn't have time to give me my massage; and when he came back to do it, that was when Satan took hold of me.

So in the evening I went to bed early, I didn't want anything; at midnight I woke up because I didn't feel well ... but I didn't call Groddeck, I got by on my own. Today I feel pretty well, although demoralised by the fact that I have gained a kilo, which Groddeck considers natural and bound up with the rest of it. I said to Groddeck that perhaps it was the family visit that disturbed me and that I had thought of asking Olga not to come ... he said I could do that, but that in the final analysis it was for my family that I had to get better and that there wouldn't, therefore, be a lot of sense in trying to avoid them.

....

... I don't like the weather we're having, with melting snow and mud; yesterday I wasn't able to go out again. Groddeck said it wasn't worth forcing me, that there was no point in taking exercise and that I should do what I wanted.

....

Groddeck has gone on an excursion into the mountains; the house is terribly silent. I told him that I spent my night wondering how it would be if I felt ill on that very night; he said that I needed only to ring and that people would come and fetch him because he wouldn't be far away.

....

127

25th January 1927

... In the morning I was very busy because, as it was Monday, Groddeck was having his Sunday in his hut; so he wasn't torturing me and my only treatment was baths; also I seized the opportunity to go out from 11 o'clock ...

....

They will certainly celebrate my birthday, so now I am racking my brains to know how I could, by way of a surprise, teach Britta to dance the csárdás ... This is how I would like to honour my country.

....

I have just met Melanie Klein's son-in-law who has just come back – the Hussar Schmideberg – at present a medical student. Perhaps I shall go out with him after dinner ...

I have just come back from the café, at 1.30, with Schmideberg; he knows Michael and Alice [Balint] well ...

26th January 1927

... Today I asked Groddeck to teach me the best way to help my intense desire to get better, because it is towards this that I would like to use my energy which is currently going to waste. But he smiled: 'Energie kann da nicht helfen.'[11]

... I intercepted Britta, the niece, in the hall and, being very mysterious, I invited her to come into my room so that I could tell her something. She was so surprised that I practically had to splash her with cold water to make her recover. Then I told her of my intention to teach her the csárdás. Of course, she is very keen to do it. But she is a little anxious about her toilette and other details, so she has asked to think it over.

... Britta has given her consent and I start lessons tomorrow. Now she is very busy making plans for the Hungarian dress ...

27th January 1927

... I am glad that you have been dancing; it seems that once again you have been aware of one of my secrets, and guess that I have enrolled here with a couple of dancing teachers ...

.... Today I once again had a long conversation with Groddeck; I was in despair about yesterday's relapse, but he smiled and corrected my erroneous conception according to which an illness should get better by following a regular progression, and he said to me, today for the first time, that he was convinced that he would dismiss me from here in six weeks in perfect health. Then he added: 'Das ist meine Ansicht, aber schliesslich ...'[12]

He has a way of speaking which is so serious and reassuring that I replied with complete conviction: 'Wenn Sie Ansicht sagen, so ist dies bei Ihnen Überzeugung, und *Ihre* Überzeugung ist mir absolut beruhigend.'[13]

Today there was ragoût of veal for lunch, of course without potatoes, gravy, or anything, and then coffee which I always drink half cold, to quench my thirst. Before lunch, I gave Britta her first lesson in the csárdás; she came through it well, I think that it will work. I only ask myself how to inculcate a bit of lightness into this cold Swede.

... I have swallowed a trout, which Groddeck immediately massaged down, then I went to listen to music with Schmideberg and we are just home, at midnight, him blind drunk, me parched ...

28th January 1927

... I have been all over the old town in all directions, with the result that I strolled around for an hour and a half before coming back to the house. It is a very pretty little town; the most beautiful thing is that there are not more than 2 or 3 streets with the houses built next to each other, the rest are villas, with beautiful big parks around them. What is most interesting is that there are a lot of southern plants mixed in with the fir trees (what a contrast!). So practically everything is green ... For my Hungarian gala costume, I had to buy myself a shirt with a soft collar which I can turn down and I also needed a record of Hungarian music; I have found one – Brahms' *Hungarian Dances* – I think that that will do the trick ...

I don't know whether I have already told you that Melanie Klein has divorced and that she has now settled in England where she is analysing children; it seems that everything is going well for her. It is Herr Klein who is living in the villa in Berlin. The mother has taken with her the youngest son, the oldest has stayed with his father in Berlin, and their only daughter, Frau Schmideberg, is, of course, in Berlin with her husband ...

....

And now ... I am going to work, to give a dancing lesson. ... With Brahms' help, things are going much better, I think that things will get animated. I have given the lady all the instructions about toilette, and my loose flowing trousers, my waistcoat with copper buttons and my paper boots are also ready ... After my poor little most un-birthday-like dinner, Groddeck poked me and beat me even more appallingly than ever, for my birthday, he said. In a rage, I rushed off to the café, and I have just come back, after 11 o'clock, with Schmideberg; I can hear Britta chuckling in the next room, it seems that she is rehearsing for tomorrow.

....

29th January 1927

....

When I came back from my bath this morning, I found in my room a splendidly decorated table, full of all sorts of plants and presents prettily arranged. A candle, with lots of red hearts painted on it, was burning brightly next to a gigantic cake on which was written: 'To the heart, with the heart, from the heart.' They have certainly copied that onto a spiced bread brought by Frau Ferenczi; on the cake, too, was a big red heart.[14] We shall know more about it this evening, when, doubtless, it will be eaten. Ah yes, I also received from the Sanatorium as a present a ceramic cigar box from Baden. Very nice. So, while I'm there admiring the table, suddenly outside the door a festive chorale bursts forth, sung by all the staff. And there was Groddeck, and Frau Groddeck, and their daughter, and their niece and Schmideberg. After the birthday serenade, they also sang a song composed especially for the occasion; the text was written by Tina, the bath lady, and she expressed the wish that Elma should read it because she absolutely adores her.

... We have splendid weather ... I am sitting down in front of the open window and am thirsting for tonight. We are invited to Frau Groddeck's – Schmideberg, too. I have ordered pork.

... I was really happy to be able to dance the csárdás; they encored us over and over again and you could see how much pleasure it was giving these very kind people that I was engaging in these antics. I tied a red ribbon round my hat, and stuck a bouquet of violets into it. And after the dance, I took off the bouquet and offered it to my partner. Of course, they asked if that was the custom among us. I said that wasn't all and, *ad demonstrandum*, I enthusiastically held the cold Swede to my bosom and planted a firm kiss on her lips ... Towards midnight, we asked if we should retire; then Groddeck said that first of all, he too wanted to dance Hungarian style, and he set himself to executing a delightful composition in his way ... He was certainly happy to know that I was on the road to recovery ... He looked at me very knowingly, because he is a very good man, and I have the impression that he likes me a lot ...

30th January 1927

... It seems that Groddeck was still in a birthday mood, because he made me make 50 respiratory movements; then he gave me such a rough time that one side still hurts me. I told him that among us, when one receives such hard blows – for he gives those too – our custom is to return them. He said that at the end, before I leave, I could do that. But I said that I would more likely want to stroke him. He really is a kind and remarkable man ...

... Ah yes! I wanted to tell you about those bizarre things which Groddeck does to me: as if he wanted to reorganise everything in me. First of all, he pushes my stomach downwards; then, as if he wanted to push it under my ribs. He has removed every sort of fat from my chest and the region of the heart. I walk around with a completely new skin; with my black moustache of yesterday, painted by myself, you would not even have recognised me.

Your letter has just arrived, my darling; I am very glad that you have at last had a letter from Ferenczi;[15] it scarcely surprises me that he holds you in such great esteem and considers you the best in Budapest; in any case it is pleasant to hear him praising you again and again and showing you his esteem.

31st January 1927

... Isn't this Groddeck adorable? As I complained a little this morning, he also came back to see me this evening, a Sunday, which is not his custom ...

1st February 1927

... I got Groddeck to tell me everything today, in clear terms. It follows that from the 17th I can leave whenever I like, even if I am not completely recovered, because the process will reach a successful conclusion at home ... Once I get there, I shall not need any further treatment. He will prescribe me a mode of living, a diet, etc., and he assures me that all will go well.

... Today, I had a real lunch: stuffed veal, savoury potatoes, an excellent vegetable and some compote, and then a sort of dark brown gelatinous substance. Some bread ...

In the evening I complained to Groddeck that I was getting too much to eat, but I have already regretted this. For dinner there was: one croquette with a tiny bit of spinach, then a sort of orange jelly in two half-peels. Tomorrow I shall withdraw my complaint.

2nd February 1927

...

In the room next door, instead of Britta,[16] it's Frau Groddeck who for the second consecutive day is looking after her flowers. She has quantities of them. Her azalea from last year is coming into bloom again ... Yesterday ... I offered her Alice's book.[17] She immediately gave me some detective novels in return ...

Now I am going to have lunch. It is true, Groddeck says that it is better to have several meals a day; for example, fruit at around 11 o'clock and in the afternoon. It seems that in this way the stomach does not expand and one is less hungry.

....

As to your anxiety about lay analysis, I believe that you are wrong, because apart from Freud, there is also Ferenczi, and he has a certain prestige, not just among those in Budapest, but also among the others ...

6th February 1927

....

Today, I had a leg bath, something rather unpleasant, because where the water at 37° stops, my skin burns badly ... I am full of pity for it because up to there it is red like roast beef.

....

Ferenczi's letters have given me great pleasure, and my optimistic self was very pleased that decent people are very fond of me ...

....

I chatted with Groddeck; then Schmideberg got me to come for a little talk, although in fact, I talk, he says nothing; he is a very inscrutable man, sparing of words, but kind; he only opens his mouth to pour something into it ...

8th February 1927

....

Today it is extremely quiet in the house; the Groddecks are in their hut, it is Monday, the substitute for Sunday. As for my friend Schmideberg, he has escaped from his bed and has not even come back for lunch.

9th February 1927

....

Fräulein Spalding arrives with great news: from the next dinner I shall be able to eat everything, in small portions, and I shall have beer instead of spritzer, even though the quantity of liquid stays the same.

11th February 1927

My little Treasure, great sensation at the sana! The *Hausdame*[18] is leaving, as soon as a suitable replacement can be found. I immediately asked Groddeck if he didn't think the position would suit Elma. He replied that he would think about it. I said that I didn't know whether she would agree to abandon her present employment to come. But I know that Elma loves being here and I thought that here at least she would get better, even though I would be sorry she was leaving Budapest. I believe that she would be absolutely suitable, she speaks several languages, she has a smart appearance and she is competent in management and book-keeping ...

13th February 1927

....

Soon there will be a great silence in the house, Frau Groddeck has already left for the hut and I believe that Groddeck will leave soon as well. But first he is coming to see me, and tomorrow I shall no doubt have another fast day because I have regained a kilo ...

Well, sadly I have lost no weight, so today I shall vegetate sadly, with just a litre of coffee ...

15th February 1927

... You know that today I am having a fast day, that I am only allowed to take a litre of liquid – any sort ... Today is the first day on which I have not experienced any unpleasant sensation while walking ... so ... I set about climbing a mountain, but I had to rest there; in short, I don't want to become a superman. I was so happy that I sent a pineapple to Groddeck, as he, at least, shall eat well. He deserves it, he is so charming, so good and so kind ... My darling, get my tobacconist to send a box of English cigarettes (round packet) if he still has any, and if he hasn't, get him to order some. Groddeck very much likes good cigarettes and you can't get them here.

I went out exploring, because it is so pleasant not to have to get back in time for lunch. Then I drank a quarter of a litre of coffee, and to complete the illusion, I followed it with a cup of black coffee. Now I am already happily smoking my cigar and, for the moment at least, I am not even hungry.

....

My conscientious fasting has had the effect of making me lose the kilo again, so that at the moment, I am once again eighty-eight and a half kilos without my clothes. It is Tuesday morning, the new week begins, in accordance with the custom here; the doctor is already back from his hut; I am curious as to what he will say about the pineapple.

....

17th February 1927

....

In the afternoon, I was getting ready to go dancing in the Casino, but unfortunately I was prevented. Fräulein Spalding came to see me, she wanted to compliment me on the half-kilo I have lost. The result was that I then went to visit Schmideberg, who is in bed to-day. The poor man really looks off-colour, although he doesn't talk about his illness ... At the sana, no one knows why the others are here; I'm the only one who tells everyone, probably so that they shouldn't imagine worse. Only Frau Groddeck – whom otherwise one sees little – gossips sometimes, but then it turns out that she has got it all wrong because she doesn't really know anything either.

20th February 1927

....

The day has passed, 11 o'clock has even struck. I announced my visit to the Groddecks, but it wasn't possible because his wife had gone out; so Groddeck came down to my room for a little private chat. The *Hausdame*[19] also happened to be there; after Groddeck had gone we invited the young lady in the next door room to play cards, until now.

And for now, I shall continue to entertain myself by reading *The Seeker of Souls*,[20] a very enjoyable book whose sequel will be published very shortly. Perhaps we should translate it for publication by Pantheon.[21]

....

21st February 1927

...Today, when I asked Groddeck, he said that it would be good if, on occasion – when I have the time – I were to come back here for a week, until this unpleasant business is completely under control ...

22nd February 1927

....

Schmideberg came to see me, he had just taken his leave ... I am reading *The Seeker of Souls* with care, there is still a good deal left; I believe that the second volume is in preparation, that there will be a sequel. I wonder whether one could envisage publishing such a thing in Budapest; there are some horrible smutty things in it, but it is very entertaining; often I laugh out loud while I'm reading.

....

Now I'm going to give a quick description, before it disappears entirely in the very depths of me, of the dinner I had five minutes ago: a cheesy thingummy in a minuscule shell – I don't know what, despite all my efforts I met nothing with enough substance to be able to chew it – then, in another little container, half a stuffed egg and a slice of raw tomato, 4 minuscule radishes, 2 ultra-fine slices of cheese, 3 spirals of butter (of which I left one) and finally a thin slice of bread.

At the moment I am waiting for coffee, and then I shall quickly light a cigar to chase away the desire to have dinner.

....

24th February 1927

....

Groddeck said to me that the physical as well as psychic causes of my illness had disappeared, so I could go home with an easy mind, and that I would be sure to feel well and to be able to walk. He had fulfilled his duty as a doctor, he could do no more for me and in any case I had no need of him. Consequently, he could offer me no more than his philosophy of life, which, however, I would henceforth merely find amusing. But if I wanted to stay for that, I could.

....

25th February 1927

My darling ... as you see, I have stayed. I had the impression that as I don't really have anything urgent to do at home, it would be better to stay here for another few days. Even though, according to Groddeck, I was done with here ...

26th February 1927

My dear little one, after the day I had yesterday, when I was edgy and unsettled because of the journey, here I am sitting in my room, calm and satisfied, and I feel well. It seems that it was a good thing to stay on a bit ... When I announced my decision to stay, Groddeck simply reacted with his habitual satanic laugh and contented himself with telling me that he was very glad about it ...

27th February 1927

....

Now, I do no more than wait for Tuesday, that will be enough for me ... The sana is beginning to fill up, I believe that there is only one free room left. But it will soon be occupied. It is around springtime that things are at their busiest here, in winter everything is calm.

....

When you read this letter, I shall be in the train; this week is irrevocably the last of my cure, here, and I am very happy to be able to see you and hear you once again, my dear Treasure, after exactly 8 weeks of absence, on Wednesday ...

[1] Diminutive of 'Frigyes', that is to say, Frédéric/Friedrich/Frederick.

[2] Translated from the German: 'She was close to dying.'

[3] In German in the text: the 'housekeeper'.

[4] A mixture of white wine and soda water.

[5] See the collection of caricatures from the Salzburg Congress, 1924.

[6] The csárdás.

[7] Groddeck's daughter, Barbara.

[8] Olga, Vilma's younger daughter, was on her way back from the USA. After stopping in Paris, her train had to pass through Baden-Baden.

[9] 'How should I know. It's you who must know best.'

[10] The Austro-Hungarian empire, which was broken up by the Treaty of Versailles after the First World War.

[11] 'Energy is of no use here.'

[12] 'That is my point of view, but if it comes to it ...'

[13] 'When you say "point of view", with you it's a conviction, and *your* conviction entirely reassures me.'

[14] The heart is a very common motif in Hungarian folklore.

[15] At this time, Ferenczi was in America.

[16] She had gone to another town to pursue her studies.

[17] Alice Bálint, *Psychoanalysis of the Nursery* (Routledge & Kegan Paul, London, 1953).

[18] In German in the text: 'housekeeper'.

[19] See previous note.

[20] A novel by Groddeck, *Der Seelensucher*.

[21] Publishing house directed by Ladislas Dormandi, one of Frédéric Kovács' sons-in-law. Groddeck's novel doesn't seem to have been published by them but they did publish the Hungarian version of *Thalassa: Essay of a Theory of Genitality* and *Psychoanalytic Notebook* by Ferenczi, as well as Alice Bálint's works.

APPENDIX 2

Chronology of Letters

Ferenczi to Groddeck: *Groddeck to Ferenczi:*

1921 (6)
26th April **New letter
17th August
24th August
Undated early letter **
23rd September ('Committee' to Groddeck)
25th December

1922 (6)   **1922** (2)
27th February
2nd May
8th May

                                           9th May **

8th July
11th October

                                             12th November

11th December

1923 (8)
19th February
4th May *New card
9th June
5th August
20th August **
16th September *
8th October
25th October

1924 (3)
30th June
11th October **
undated card for New Year *

140

Ferenczi to Groddeck:

Groddeck to Ferenczi:

1925 (8)
undated *
18th April
undated *
26th July *
5th September *
10th September *
13th September
6th December

1926 (6)
7th January
27th March (misdated as 6th March 1927
in earlier editions)
26th June
26th July
30th August
13th October

1927 (2)
26th April
25th October

1928 (2)
27th July
17th October

1929 (4)
12th February

7th July
16th August
28th October

1929 (1)

13th June

Ferenczi to Groddeck: *Groddeck to Gizella:*

1930 (2)
15th June
21st December

1931 (5)
10th October
17th October *
21st October
26th October *
3rd November

1932 (1)
3rd March

1933 (1)
20th March

Gizella Ferenczi to Groddecks (2)
14th July **
2nd November **

1934 (2)   **1934** (1)
9th January 1934 **

                                  19th February (to Gizella)

28th February 1934
(to Georg Groddeck) **

Total Letters:
53 letters (and cards) Ferenczi to Groddeck
1 card from the 'Committee' (includes Ferenczi) to Groddeck
3 letters Groddeck to Ferenczi
1 letter Groddeck to Gizella Ferenczi
4 letters Gizella Ferenczi to Groddecks

Textual Notes

(Further additions, omissions, misreadings, translation queries, etc., not mentioned in the editorial notes or Chronology of Letters).

p.10, line 10: previous editions read 'when I was garrisoned (for a year)'.

p.11: 'dürren' [arid, bare, barren], (3rd paragraph, 2nd line), omitted in previous editions – misread as 'diesen'.

p.20, 2nd line: Ferenczi appears to write 'in ½ an hour' – previous editions read 'in ¼ of an hour'. We have used the latter reading in this edition.

p.25: Gizella's postscript, which was omitted in previous editions, added.

p.32: Gizella's postscript omitted in previous editions.

pp.34-37: Groddeck's November 12th, 1922 letter translated from published German edition (Fischer Verlag) – facsimile missing.

p.45: Sándor's greetings to Frau Emmy here added; last two sentences of Sándor's postscript were also omitted in previous editions.

p.52: lines 4, 5, and 7 omitted in previous editions.

pp.55-56: postscripts by Gizella and Elma omitted in previous editions.

p.81: Gizella's postscript, dated 27th October, in Ferenczi's letter of 25th October, added.

p.85: Gizella's postscript omitted in previous editions.

p.91: first four lines omitted in previous editions.

p.98: Gizella's postscript omitted in previous editions.

Bibliography

PRIMARY SOURCES

Letters of Gizella Ferenczi, Elma Laurvik, and Sarolta Altschul
Freud–Ferenczi letters
Ferenczi–Rank letters (Rank Papers – Columbia University)
M. Severn letters
British Psycho-Analytical Society papers
Ferenczi–Jones correspondence
Balint archive papers
Groddeck sanatorium guestbook
Groddeck Society papers
Groddeck archive (Deutsches Literaturarchiv Marbach).

Abbreviations used for Ferenczi's Collected Works

C. *First Contributions to Psychoanalysis*. Trans. Ernest Jones. London: Hogarth Press, 1952. Reprinted London: Karnac, 1994.

F.C. *Further Contributions to the Theory and Technique of Psychoanalysis*. Compiled by J. Rickman. Trans. Jane Suttie and others. London: Hogarth Press, 1926 (2nd ed., 1950). Reprinted London: Karnac, 1994.

Fin. *Final Contributions to the Problems and Methods of Psychoanalysis*. Ed. M. Balint. Trans. Eric Mosbacher and others. London: Hogarth Press/ New York: Basic Books, 1955. Reprinted London: Karnac, 1994.

WORKS BY FERENCZI AND GRODDECK

Ferenczi's Writings

Ferenczi, S. (1899). 'Spiritism'. See *Sándor Ferenczi: Selected Writings*, pp.3-8. (Ed. Julia Borossa, London, Penguin Books, 1999).
_____(1909). 'Introjection and transference.' C. pp.35-93.
_____(1911a). 'On obscene words.' C. pp.132-153.
_____(1911b). 'On the organization of the psycho-analytic movement.' Fin. pp.299-307.
_____(1913a). 'A little Chanticleer.' C. pp.240-252.
_____(1913b) 'Flatus as an adult prerogative.' F.C. p.325
_____(1914). 'On the ontogenesis of the interest in money.' C. pp.319-331.

_____(1916/17). 'Disease- or patho-neuroses.' F.C. pp.78-89.

_____(1917). Review of *Psychische Bedingtheit und psychoanalytische Behandlung organischer Leiden* by Georg Groddeck (Psychic Conditioning and the Psychoanalytic Treatment of Organic Disorders). Fin. pp.342-343.

_____(1919a). 'Disgust for breakfast.' F.C. p.326.

_____(1919b). 'Technical difficulties in the analysis of a case of hysteria.' F.C. pp.189-197.

_____(1921a). 'The further development of an active therapy in psycho-analysis.' F.C. pp.198-217.

_____(1921b). Review of Georg Groddeck's *Der Seelensucher*. Ein psycho-analytischer Roman. First pub. in German in *Imago* (1921) 7, p.356. Fin. pp.344-348.

_____(c.1921). 'On epileptic fits: observations and reflections.' Fin. pp.197-204.

_____(1923). 'The dream of the 'clever baby.' F.C. pp.349-350.

_____(1924). *Thalassa: A Theory of Genitality*. London: Karnac, 1989. (Versuch einer Genitaltheorie. Vienna: Internationaler Psycho-analytischer Verlag, 1924, and New York: *Psychoanalytic Quarterly*, 1938).

_____(1925). 'Contra-indications to the "active" psycho-analytical technique.' F.C. pp.217-230.

_____(1926a). 'Gulliver phantasies.' Fin. pp.41-60.

_____(1926b). 'Organ neuroses and their treatment.' Fin. pp.22-28.

_____(1928). 'The elasticity of psycho-analytic technique.' Fin. pp.87-101.

_____ (1930a). 'Masculine and feminine.' In *The Psychoanalytic Review*, 17: pp.105-113.

_____(1930b). 'The principle of relaxation and neocatharsis.' Fin. pp.108-125.

_____(1920, 1930-32). 'Notes and fragments.' Fin. pp.216-279.

_____(1931). 'Child analysis in the analysis of adults.' Fin. pp.126-142.

_____(1932). *The Clinical Diary of Sándor Ferenczi*. Ed. J. Dupont (trans. M. Balint and N.Z. Jackson). Cambridge, MA: Harvard University Press, 1988. (Orig. publ. as *Journal Clinique*, Paris: Payot, 1985.)

_____(1933). 'Confusion of tongues between adults and the child.' Fin. pp.156-167.

Ferenczi, S.

_____and Hollós, I. (1922). *Zur Psychoanalyse der paralytischen Geistes-störung*, Leipzig. In English: *Psychoanalysis and the Psychic Disorder of General Paresis* (1925). New York: Nervous and Mental Disease Publ. Co.

_____and Rank, O. (1924). *The Development of Psycho-Analysis*. New York: Nervous and Mental Disease Publ. Co., 1925.

Groddeck's Writings

Groddeck, G. (1909). *Hin zu Gottnatur* (Towards God Nature).
Leipzig: S. Hirzel. Untranslated.

_____(1913). *Nasamecu, natura sanat, medicus curat.* Der gesunde und
kranke Mensch (The healthy and sick person). Leipzig: S. Hirzel.
Untranslated.

_____(1921a). *Der Seelensucher.* Ein psychoanalytischer Roman (The
Seeker of Souls: A Psychoanalytic Novel). Vienna/Leipzig: Internationaler Psychoanalytischer Verlag.

_____(1921b). 'On psychoanalysing the organic in human beings.' (Über die
Psychoanalyse des Organischen im Menschen.) *Internationale Zeitschrift für Psychoanalyse,* 7.

_____(1923). *The Book of the It* (Das Buch vom Es). London: Vision Press,
1950; New York: Vintage 1961. Originally published Vienna/Leipzig:
Internationaler Psychoanalytischer Verlag, 1923.

_____(1923). 'Die Flucht in die Philosophie.' (The flight into philosophy).
International Journal of Psychoanalysis, 4: pp.373.

_____(1925). 'The It and Psychoanalysis.' *Die Arche* 1, No. 10: pp.1-15.
Reprinted in *Psychoanalytishe Schriften zur Psychosomatik* (Psycho-
analytic Papers on Psychomatics, Ed. G. Clauser. Wiesbaden: Limes
Verlag, 1964.)

_____(1929). 'Psychical Treatment of Organic Disease.' *The British Journal
of Medical Psychology,* 9 (11): pp.179-186.

_____ (1933). *Der Mensch als Symbol: Unmassgebliche Meinungen über
Sprache und Kunst* (Man as Symbol: Unauthoritative Views on
Language and Art), Vienna/Leipzig: Internationaler Psychoanalytischer
Verlag. Partially reprinted in *Psychoanalytische Schriften zur Literatur
und Kunst.* Wiesbaden: Limes Verlag, 1973.

_____ (1977). *The Meaning of Illness: Selected Psychoanalytic Writings,
including his correspondence with Sigmund Freud.* (Ed. L. Schacht.
Translated by Gertrud Mander). London: Hogarth Press; reprinted
Karnac, 1988).

WORKS BY OTHER AUTHORS

Aron, L. and Harris, A. (eds.) (1993). *The Legacy of Sándor Ferenczi.*
Hillsdale, New Jersey: The Analytic Press.

Balint, M. (1949). Sándor Ferenczi. *Int. J. Psycho-Anal.,* 30 (4), pp.215-19.

_____(1951). Review of *The Book of the It. Int. J. Psycho-Anal.,* 32,
pp.250-251.

_____(1958). 'Sándor Ferenczi's last years.' (Letter to the editor). *Int. J.
Psycho-Anal.,* 39 (5), p.68.

_____(1968). *The Basic Fault: Therapeutic Aspects of Regression*. London: Tavistock Publications.

Bergmann, M. and Hartman, F. (eds.) (1976). *The Evolution of Psychoanalytic Technique*. New York: Basic Books.

Bos, J. (1992). 'On the origin of the id (das Es).' *Int. Rev. Psycho-Anal.* 19, pp.433-443.

Breuer, J. and Freud, S. (1895). *Studies on Hysteria*. Standard Edition, 2, pp.1-305.

Chasseguet-Smirgel, J. (1985). *The Ego Ideal: A Psychoanalytic Essay on the Malady of the Ideal*. New York: Norton.

Cocks, G. (1985). *Psychotherapy in the Third Reich*. New York/Oxford: Oxford University Press.

de Forest, I. (1954). *The Leaven of Love*. New York: Da Capo Press.

Dupont, J. (1988). Introduction: *The Clinical Diary of Sándor Ferenczi*. Ed. J. Dupont (transl. M. Balint and N.Z. Jackson). Cambridge, MA: Harvard University Press. (Orig. publ. as *Journal Clinique*. Paris: Payot, 1985).

_____(1994a). 'Freud's analysis of Ferenczi as revealed by their correspondence.' *Int. J. Psycho-Anal.*, 75, pp.301-320.

_____ (1994b). 'The Notion of Trauma according to Ferenczi: Progress or Regression in Psychoanalytic Theory?' In *100 Years of Psychoanalysis* (Cahiers Psychiatriques Genevois, special issue), Eds. A. Haynal and E. Falzeder. Geneva: Institutions Universitaires de Psychiatrie de Genève, pp.205-215.

Eagle, M. (1984). 'Psychoanalysis and modern psychodynamic theories'. In *Personality and the Behaviour Disorders* (Revised edition). Eds. N. Endler and J. Hunt. New York: John Wiley.

_____(1987). *Recent Developments in Psychoanalysis: A Critical Evaluation*. Cambridge, MA: Harvard University Press.

Ellenberger, H. (1970). *The Discovery of the Unconscious*. New York: Basic Books.

Emde, R. (1988). Development terminable and interminable. II. Recent psychoanalytic theory and therapeutic considerations. *Int. J. Psycho-Anal.*, 69: pp.283-296.

Fortune, C. (1993). 'The case of RN: Sándor Ferenczi's radical experiment in psychoanalysis.' In *The Legacy of Sándor Ferenczi*. Eds. L. Aron and A. Harris. Hillsdale, NJ: The Analytic Press, pp.101-120.

_____(1994). 'A difficult ending: Ferenczi, "R.N.", and the experiment in mutual analysis.' In *100 Years of Psychoanalysis* (Cahiers Psychiatriques Genevois, special issue). Eds. A. Haynal and E. Falzeder. Geneva: Institutions Universitaires de Psychiatrie de Genève, pp.217-223.

_____ (1996). 'Mutual analysis: a logical outcome of Sándor Ferenczi's experiments in psychoanalysis.' In *Ferenczi's Turn in Psycho-analysis*. Ed. P. Rudnytsky. New York: New York University Press, pp.170-186.

Freud, S. (1896). 'The aetiology of hysteria.' Standard Edition, 3.

_____(1911). 'Psycho-analytic notes upon an autobiographical account of a case of paranoia (Dementia Paranoides).' Standard Edition, 12, 3-82.

_____(1912). *Totem and Taboo*. Standard Edition, 13, 1-161.

_____(1914). 'On the history of the psychoanalytic movement.' Standard Edition, 14.

_____(1923a). *The Ego and the Id*. Standard Edition, 19.

_____(1923b). 'Two encyclopaedia articles.' Standard Edition, 18.

_____(1925). 'Negation.' Standard Edition. 19

_____(1937). 'Analysis terminable and interminable.' Standard Edition, 23.

_____and Ferenczi, S. (1993). *The Correspondence of Sigmund Freud and Sándor Ferenczi*, Vol. I, 1908-1914. Eds. E. Brabant, E. Falzeder, and P. Giampieri-Deutsch (trans. P. Hoffer). Cambridge, MA.: Harvard University Press/ Belknap.

_____and Ferenczi, S. (1996). *The Correspondence of Sigmund Freud and Sándor Ferenczi*, Vol. II, 1915-1919. Eds. E. Falzeder, E. Brabant, and P. Giampieri-Deutsch (trans. P. Hoffer). Cambridge, MA.: Harvard University Press/ Belknap.

_____and Ferenczi, S. (2000). *The Correspondence of Sigmund Freud and Sándor Ferenczi*, Vol. III, 1920-1933. Eds. E. Falzeder, E. Brabant, and P. Giampieri-Deutsch (trans. P. Hoffer). Cambridge, MA.: Harvard University Press/ Belknap.

_____and Groddeck, see Groddeck, 1977, above.

_____and Jones, E. (1993). *The Complete Correspondence of Sigmund Freud and Ernest Jones 1908-1939*. Ed. R.A. Paskauskas. Cambridge, MA.: Harvard University Press/Belknap.

_____and Jung, C.G. (1974). *The Freud/Jung Letters*: The Correspondence between Sigmund Freud and C.G. Jung, ed. W. McGuire. Transl. Ralph Manheim and R.F.C. Hull. Princeton: Bollingen.

Gill, M. (1984). 'Psychoanalysis and psychotherapy: A revision.' *Int. Rev. Psycho-Anal.* 11: pp.161-179.

Grosskurth, P. (1991). *The Secret Ring: Freud's Inner Circle and the Politics of Psycho-Analysis*. Reading, Mass: Addison-Wesley.

Grossman, C. and Grossman, S. (1965). *The Wild Analyst*. New York: George Braziller.

Grubrich-Simitis, I. (1986). 'Six letters of Sigmund Freud and Sándor Ferenczi on the interrelationship of psychoanalytic theory and technique.' *Int. Rev. Psycho-Anal.*, 13: pp.1-19.

Haynal, A. (1988). *The Technique at Issue: Controversies in Psychoanalysis from Freud and Ferenczi to Michael Balint*. London: Karnac.

149

_____(1993). 'Ferenczi and the origins of psychoanalytic technique'. In *The Legacy of Sándor Ferenczi*. Eds. L. Aron and A. Harris. Hillsdale, New Jersey: The Analytic Press, pp.53-74.

_____and Falzeder, E. (1991). 'Healing through love? A unique dialogue in the history of psychoanalysis.' Part I, *Free Associations*, 2 (21), pp.1-20.

Hidas, G. (1993). 'Flowing over – transference, countertransference, telepathy: subjective dimensions of the psychoanalytic relationship in Ferenczi's thinking.' In *The Legacy of Sándor Ferenczi*. Eds. L. Aron and A. Harris. Hillsdale, NJ: The Analytic Press. pp.207-215.

Hoffer, A. (1996) Introduction to *The Correspondence of Sigmund Freud and Sándor Ferenczi*, Vol. II. Eds. E. Falzeder and E. Brabant (trans. P. Hoffer). Cambridge, MA: Harvard University Press/Belknap.

Hollós, I. (1926). *Hinter der gelben Mauer* (Farewell to the Yellow House). *Mes adieux à la maison jaune* (Paris: Le Coq Heron, no. 100.)

Jones, E. (1957). *Sigmund Freud: Life and Work*. Vol. 3. London: Hogarth.

Kardiner, A. (1977). *My Analysis with Freud: Reminiscences*. New York: Norton.

LaPlanche, J. and Pontalis, J. B. (1988). *The Language of Psycho-Analysis*. London: Hogarth Press.

Lorin, C. (1983). *Le Jeune Ferenczi: Premiers Ecrits 1899-1906*. Paris: Aubier Montaigne.

Mitchell, S. (1993). *Hope and Dread in Psychoanalysis*. New York: Basic Books.

Modell, A. (1991). 'A confusion of tongues or whose reality is it?' *Psychoanalytic Quarterly*. LX, pp.227-244.

Molnar, M. (1992). *The Diary of Sigmund Freud: 1929-1939*. New York: Scribners.

Oberndorf, C. (1953). *A History of Psychoanalysis in America*. New York: Grune & Stratton.

Popper, K. (1989). *Conjectures and Refutations: The Growth of Scientific Knowledge*. London: Routledge.

Quinn, S. (1988). *A Mind of Her Own: The Life of Karen Horney*. New York: Addison-Wesley.

Radó, S. (1927). 'Das Problem der Melancholie.' *Int. Zeitschrift für Psychoanalyse*. Vol. 9 (4), October 1928, pp. 420-38.

Rank, O. (1929). *The Trauma of Birth*. New York: Harcourt, Brace. German edition: Int. Psychoanalytischer Verlag, Vienna/Leipzig, 1924.

Roazen, P. and Swerdloff, B. (1995). *Heresy: Sándor Radó and the Psychoanalytic Movement*. Northvale, New Jersey, and London: Jason Aronson.

Romm, S. (1983). *The Unwelcome Intruder: Freud's Struggle with Cancer*. New York: Praeger.

Roustang, F. (1982). *Dire Mastery: Discipleship from Freud to Lacan.* Baltimore, MD: Johns Hopkins University.

Rycroft, C. (1972). *A Critical Dictionary of Psychoanalysis.* Harmondsworth: Penguin.

Sabourin, P. (1985). *Ferenczi: Paladin et Grand Vizir Secret.* Paris: Editions Universitaires.

Salomé, L. (1987). *The Freud Journal.* London: Quartet Books.

Schur, M. (1972). *Freud: Living and Dying.* New York: International Universities Press.

Severn, E. (1933). *The Discovery of the Self.* London: Rider.

Simmel, E. (1926). 'Georg Groddeck on the occasion of his sixtieth birthday.' *Int. Zeitschrift,* 12: pp.591-595.

Stanton, M. (1990). *Sándor Ferenczi: Reconsidering Active Intervention.* London: Free Association Books and Northvale, NJ: Jason Aronson, 1991.

Weiss, J., Sampson, H. and the Mount Zion Psychotherapy Research Group. (1986). *The Psychoanalytic Process.* New York: Guilford Press.

Whan, M. (1987). 'Chiron's wound: some reflections on the wounded healer.' *Chiron: A Review of Jungian Analysis.*

Will, H. (1994). 'Ferenczi und Groddeck. Eine Freundschaft.' *Psyche* XLVIII 8: pp.720-737.

Winnicott, D. (1958). *Collected Papers: Through Pediatrics to Psycho-analysis.* New York: Basic Books.

151

Index